PRAISE

for *How to Build a Stewardship
Church That Loves the Poor*

"This book takes stewardship from dream to pastoral reality. It is a concrete response to the challenges of stewardship building in every community.

A 'must book' for a growing parish."

—Most Rev. Rolando Octavus J. Tria Tirona, OCD, DD,
Archbishop of Caceres, Naga City

"Thank you very much for this *hulog ng langit* (godsend) and a much-needed formation guide on such a timely topic—so fitting a gift for our 500 Years of Christianity celebration!

I not only endorse it to be used in the whole Diocese of San Carlos but everywhere and anywhere where Church leadership humbly recognizes we have failed, been distracted, or even lost our Church vision and mission of making disciples and is now committed to building a Stewardship Church that Loves the Poor!"

—Most Rev. Gerardo A. Alminaza, DD,
Bishop of San Carlos, Negros Occidental

Taking a fresh, practical approach, Jose Luis Clemente offers us a singularly reliable resource for implementing stewardship in a parish. His work should be added to that "core curriculum" that explains how stewardship enhances our Catholic life of faith.

—Michael Murphy,
Executive Director
International Catholic Stewardship Council,
U.S.A.

"This is a hard-hitting masterpiece on alternative methods and approaches of New Evangelization. It clearly and poetically captured the reflective witnessing and living experience of the spirituality of stewardship.

May all pastors and lay leaders of our church read this inspiring book!"

—Fr. Noel Conopio,
Director of Diocesan Social Action Center
Pondo ng Pinoy Diocesan Desk
and Administrator of Bahay-Pari,
Diocese of San Pablo

"Stewardship is Life! A good and faithful Christian keeps on doing stewardship in good times and bad, amidst all adversities. This book—a piece of art—will help the reader navigate the challenges and trials of doing stewardship in the Church. I fully recommend walking through its pages, especially those who would like to make stewardship a way of life."

—Fr. Manuel Vicente Catral,
Parish Priest of San Pedro Telmo Parish,
Aparri, Cagayan

"A timely guide to our quest to infuse vibrant life to our faith as we move beyond 500 Years of Christianity in the Philippines."

—Fr. Leonardo Dublan Jr.,
Parish Priest of St. Joseph the Worker Parish,
Davao City

"How to Build a Stewardship Church that Loves the Poor came from Jose Luis Clemente's many years of experience as a Church Builder. This book is surely a great help to strengthen the Stewardship Program in parishes and make disciples who care for humanity and all creation."

—Sr. Tillie Z. Dizon, SMCC,
BEC Community Organizer,
Vicariate of Sto. Tomas de Villanueva,
Diocese of Pasig

"While the pandemic has turned things upside down in the world, the faithful may wish to consider getting a few potent ideas from Jose Luis Clemente's stewardship manual that could actually turn the Church right side up and, perhaps, the entire world on a new life-giving path."

—Br. Armin A. Luistro, FSC,
President of De La Salle University
and Former Secretary of the Department of Education,
Philippines

"The seven steps promoted in this book is an effective guide for the parish priest and his team in forming the parish into a communion of communities that is inspired by the spirituality of stewardship and that realizes the vision of a renewed Church of Vatican II and PCP II: the Church as a community of disciples living in communion; participating in the mission of Christ as priestly, prophetic, and servant/kingly people; and, as the Church of the Poor.

I highly recommend this book to the clergy and their lay and religious collaborators."

—Fr. Amado L. Picardal, CSsR,
Executive Co-Secretary
JPIC Commission-USG/UISG,
Rome, Italy

"Once you read this book, you will realize that stewardship is not just a personal mission but a communal endeavor that will compassionately build the Church of and for the Poor."

—Most Rev. Mylo Hubert C. Vergara, DD,
Bishop of Diocese of Pasig

HOW TO BUILD A STEWARDSHIP CHURCH THAT LOVES THE POOR

A Field Guide for Church Builders

Jose Luis Clemente

Edited by Katherine S. Clemente
Cover photo by Nil Buan
Cover design by Katherine S. Clemente

Library of Congress Control Number: 2018675309
Printed in the United States of America

DEDICATION

To all the priests and lay leaders who built
stewardship churches that love the poor
in the Philippines,
As much as this book belongs to me,
it most certainly belongs to you.

To Fr. Andrew Kemberling and Mila Glodava,
St. Thomas More and St. Vincent de Paul Parishes,
and the International Catholic Stewardship Council,
Like a fragrant distilled spirit,
your gift of stewardship is as intoxicating today
as it was 20 years ago.

To Fr. Nonong Pili and my betters at SPI,
For taking me to the Origin
of inspiration and melodic song,
I am astounded and grateful.

To my wife and editor, Katherine,
You are the gathered leaves
on which I sit and rest
from life's weal and woe.

CONTENTS

PREFACE

I TAKE OFF MY HAT and give high praise to the pioneer builders of stewardship churches that love the poor in the Philippines. They went to a place where few dared to go—the integral revitalization of our churches—and returned with something consequential to proclaim and share with anyone who would stop and listen.

Experiences, insights, and learnings that remain nameless and unvoiced dissipate and evanesce into the cold air of the aloof night. If left unremembered and unshared, so too would the pioneers' daring explorations fade to oblivion unsettling nothing, transforming no one.

How to Build a Stewardship Church that Loves the Poor is a modest attempt to preserve the pioneer builders' experience so we may give it a fair crack at proper "telling" hither and yon. It rounds up their best practices in transforming the church and recalibrates them into a step-by-step procedure that can help aspiring church builders realize a supercharged church that excels at making disciples who care for humanity and all creation.

This Field Guide is written especially for bishops, parish priests, and lay leaders who want to breathe new life into their churches. If you are a mover and a shaker, a man or woman of action who wants to revivify the church so that she is worthy of her Great Commission, then this book is for you.

Now here's the rub.

The challenge to capture the vastness and complexity of the pioneers' experience and to distill it to a few sharp blades of insight is a daunting task that is bound to fail. How can one measure the decades-long struggles of a parish or a diocese to renew herself? How can one judge parish priests who put their hearts and souls to the revitalization of the church but foundered and flopped in the end?

It is a chilling task that pushed me to the outer limits of my competence.

Notwithstanding my impediments, I proceeded. I knew their stories must be told even if the best that I could do was to tell them imperfectly.

Let me, therefore, say aloud what each already knows—the pioneer builders of stewardship churches that love the poor are the true custodians of their stories and truths. This book is but an imperfect snapshot, a simple two-dimensional approximation of their journey to reinvigorate the house of God.

Simply put, there are far more things to fathom and admire about their adventure than are in this book. This Field Guide is to make sure that at a minimum, a snippet of their meanings and truths is preserved and made known lest our silence and neglect come to testify against us from the mouths of our children.

If you find something here that magnifies your spirit, it is because this writer was on the nose about some things of import in the pioneers' journey. If there are portions of this book that do not inspire, it is because I failed to make it a worthy crucible of their discoveries and constitutive insights.

FOREWORDS

by Most Rev. Broderick S. Pabillo, DD and Rev. Andrew Kemberling

THE PANDEMIC HAS BROUGHT TO THE FORE that we are not owners. People are losing their jobs, losing their businesses, and even losing their prospects for the future. Suddenly, we lose control of many things in our life. This is a glorious reminder that what we have is just entrusted to us and can, thus, be taken away. We are not owners—we are only stewards and caretakers. I pray we all wise up to this truth.

Stewardship is a spirituality and a way of life. It is revealed in how we relate to people, things, and opportunities. As stewards, we manage our blessings in the name of the rightful owner. We hold that everything comes from God and, by his Providence, he has entrusted to us our life, our time, our family, our talents, our money, and our properties to mind and care for.

We should not squander or lose His bestowals but nurture them. We should consult Him about how He wants us to use our good fortunes and blessings. God has entrusted them to us so that they may serve others: We are trustees for the good of others. So "ownership" is more of a responsibility rather than a privilege. There will come a time—we do not know when—when we will have to give an account to the actual Owner and Source of what is good, of how trustworthy we were as stewards.

Stewardship in the church already has a long history—we are not starting from scratch. There have been parishes and dioceses in the Philippines and abroad which have been promoting stewardship for decades. This manual has gleaned from these experiences.

I thank Mr. Jose Luis Clemente for coming out with his manual on the how-to of stewardship as a helpful aid to the program in our parishes and religious communities. We can learn from their experiences. I hope we can make use of some ideas and practices described here.

Stewardship Programs must be promoted so that our faithful can adopt the spirituality of stewardship. Stewardship is a key teaching from the Scriptures and, by promoting it, we are evangelizing the people—making them true to who they are as God intended them to be. The purpose of this manual is not only to put in place another program in the parish but to give practical ways to live as stewards of God's care for all.

+Broderick S. Pabillo, DD
Head of the Episcopal Office on Stewardship,
Bishop of Apostolic Vicariate of Taytay, Palawan

ECCLESIOLOGY IS THE STUDY of the church. Sharing a common understanding of how to build up the church takes cooperation and goodwill. It is a privilege for me to have a shared Ecclesiology with the Church in the Philippines.

There was plenty of cooperation and goodwill from those involved to advance the Church to where our dear Lord wants us to be. I am grateful that I had the amazing opportunity to help, especially from the United States and the Church of Northern Colorado. The Philippines is on the other side of the world, but we listened to the Holy Spirit to forge a common vision that includes a working consideration for God's Holy Poor.

The Spirituality of Stewardship opened hearts and minds to hearing and seeing the Gospel. Putting God and His people created in His image first—above "things"— is simple but hard to do. The "attitude of gratitude" moved us to see everything as a gift—a gift received from God and given in return to God out of gratitude. This simple formula has been instrumental in how a Stewardship Church loves the poor.

The cooperation of Jose Luis Clemente and Socio-Pastoral Institute was instrumental in furthering this approach. The cooperation of Bishops and clergy was foundational. The teaching authority of the Philippines' local Churches is how this approach has taken root and continues to grow.

I am grateful that these servants of God serve our Lord so faithfully. When more and more lay faithful embrace this approach, the World will see a vision of the Church unseen before. The Poor will share their wisdom in a way the rest of the world needs to hear. With it, souls will be saved and the mission of the Church will be accomplished.

Rev. Andrew Kemberling
Former Chairman of the Board
International Catholic Stewardship Council, USA

PRELUDE TO THE JOURNEY

WE SAIL UNDER FALSE COLORS when we proclaim our commitment to winged purposes but refuse to pull out all the stops and do the donkeywork to realize them. Everyone and his dog say that transformation of our churches matters a great deal, but many find this heroic task not worth braving troubled water. No coincidence that a lot of our leaders don't even take a fair whack at it.

Some who sallied forth expected to win the prize in a canter without overcoming larger-than-life struggles. When they faced challenges, they jumped ship and moved on to easier things.

Regrettably, even some of our most determined leaders—the ones who nailed church renewal to their masts—came to the end of the tether. Now, that is really disturbing!

Without doubt, the road to a revitalized church is fraught with hardships, pitfalls, and dangers. If you don't know the highways and byways of transformational change like the back of your hand, you will lose your way and fall between the cracks. It is on that account that this quest has vanquished even the best of our leaders and turned most of us into perjurers or do-nothings.

Thus, this *Field Guide* on how to build a stewardship church that loves the poor.

This book is a road map to help you—the resolute traveler— mug up so you can avoid the pitfalls along the way. Contrary to persistent rumors, building a stewardship church is not an errand for fools. This book will show you the chink in the wall so you can haul yourself up to realize the Stewardship Programs of Time, Talent, and Treasure.

But the journey doesn't end there.

Building a stewardship church is a hard act to follow. This book enjoins you to keep going and do something extreme: It exhorts you to bottom-side-up the church and shift its gravity so that it favors the poor. Fair warning, the plot to build the Church of the Poor—a church that uplifts the downtrodden and the oppressed—is rarely realized that many think it a quest akin to finding a mare's nest. When asked about the Church of the Poor, many church leaders say, "I'll believe it when I see it." Or "I've never been there, but the postcards look nice."

That is where this bus is going.

For what reasons?

First, Jesus cares for the poor. They are in the front and center of why he came to this earth. This is Jesus's mission statement according to the Scriptures: "The Spirit of the Lord is upon me, because he has anointed me to preach good news to the poor. He has sent me to proclaim release to the captives and recovering of sight to the blind, to set at liberty those who are oppressed, to proclaim the acceptable year of the Lord" (Luke 4:18-19, RSV-CE).

Second, PCP II or the Second Plenary Council of the Philippines adopted the *Church of the Poor* as her official vision of a church renewed.

The Council is a representation of the entire Philippine Church. It convened in Manila in 1991 to align the Philippine Church with the spirit, acts, and decrees of Vatican II. The Council members grappled with the prodigious quandary that building a revivified church marked by *communion, participation, and mission* is impracticable when a whole slew of our brothers and sisters is impoverished, excluded, and unable to live life in its fullness. After mulling this perplexity for over a month, they concluded that the only roadway to a revitalized church, a church that is truly a community of disciples, is by helping the oppressed and poverty-stricken overcome structural evil—power arrangements, laws, and policies, to name a few—that prevent them from realizing their fullest human potential.

For the church to resuscitate herself, therefore, she must become a credible evangelizer in a context where many of our brothers and sisters are poor. **She must become a proponent of human liberation—a Church of the Poor!**

What is the promised prize waiting for us at this hard journey's end?

Simply this: A worshiping, serving, giving, and welcoming church; a church that practices preferential love for the poor; a church that lifts the poor from material and spiritual poverty; a church that relies on the poor as her primary evangelizers; a church marked by communion, participation, and mission; a church that takes part in the inbreaking of God's reign.

A church renewed.

Are you willing to break lances for this winged purpose? Is this something you take to heart? Is this new way of being church worth the protracted, bloody struggle? Will it move you to take the field?

Or not?

CAST-IRON GRIT

The road to victory is bloody and steep, so only the ones with the stoutest hearts will answer the call to adventure. In order to succeed, we need pastors who have the audacity and nerve to push the church to do the right thing despite exorbitant personal costs and the high likelihood of failure. Whether you give two straws about it or not, failure is a shadow that is with us at all times. It is with us when we champion small endeavors, like the beautification of the church; it is likewise with us when we sponsor big changes, like lay empowerment or building small Christian communities.

Surmising that the only way to avoid failure is by not taking action, many feeble leaders choose this facetious option. And since the laity regards clerics as unfailing über-men who are bona fide members of the very exclusive tribe of the wisest of wise, these pastors then view failure as a genuine nightmare and her nine-fold. So, at the very first sign of trouble, they surrender their lofty goals because failure is a cunning thief who can quickly rob them of their illumination of infallibility.

Accordingly, they refuse to roll the dice for risky projects such as church renewal.

In opposition, there are cast-iron leaders who will do everything to realize their loftiest dreams for church and society. They have boundless fortitude and determination to forge forward no matter what; they soldier on and carry any burden no matter how heavy; they pay any price no matter how steep—all for the sake of victory. **These champions persevere in the face of failure, buoyed up by mother wit that failures are stepping stones to victory.** Unlike fragile leaders who throw up the sponge when the going gets tough, they are not afraid of failure, because they consider growing, learning, and becoming their stock-in-trade.

Not ego.

Rather than bending the knee to adversity and defeat, these champions use them as an appliance to extract the best from their beings. They employ disappointments like hard-nosed Sherpas to carry them to the mountaintops where the air is rarefied but the majestic view continual. Faced with ruin and danger, they shout, "*Stay the course!*" and they hold the fort with everything they could muster—come hell or high water.

By choosing growth over the safety of their egos, by never giving up on their dreams, by convincing themselves that God is on their side, they indubitably win. That is how these exceptional leaders "stumble and fail" their way to eventual success.

It is this unbreakable determination that separates cracked-hand winners from most who are but starry-eyed dreamers and losers.

Beware, therefore, of the run-of-the-mill parish priest who claims commitment to the highest ideals yet settles for the cheapest, easiest, nearest, or good enough. He will pass and sit this vision quest out. Do not trust the ones who talk big game but refuse to play it, who have one foot in the hunt and another foot out. Do not rely on leaders who spend their days studying, watching, debating, speculating, and dithering behind air-conditioned walls. They will only bring you to rack and ruin.

This is the palpable in the quest—walk only with the most determined.

Go only with *one of ten thousand.*

EXPERTISE AND SKILL

What is not plain as the nose on your face is that, aside from a stout heart, one needs pastors with the competencies of tip-top managers. I refer here to leaders who can facilitate the *planning, implementation, monitoring, and evaluation cycles* that enable the church to realize her highest purposes. Minus this bread and water competency, one has but a ghost of a chance to build a stewardship church.

Never mind a Church of the Poor.

Hold this dear—any tinpot leader can, for a moment, make things that dazzle like shooting stars; however, only the ones with solid management skills can create institutional changes, programs, and initiatives that you can hang your hat on.

We need pastors who can turn the proper organizational valves, gears, and levers so that the church can achieve its highest institutional goals and ambitions. **Without a solid aptitude on how to manage projects, programs, and ministries, even bound and determined parish priests will fall by the wastelands and crash down like lead balloons.**

Here are some of the familiar codas and refrains, a few repeating words in this sad but popular song on failure brought by managerial incompetence:

The parish priest sponsors a new program but does not invest enough funds or put the right people to lead it. They launch the program amid great fanfare, but after plodding along for a year, the initiative shudders and bites the dust.

How about the project that started strong but ran out of steam because the pastor declared victory too early? He failed to consolidate and build on the gains of the early wins to create momentum.

And remember the parish priest who focused on the *what* of the project and neglected the *why*? The project took off like a rocket but was soon in tatters. For what reason? Because he failed to inspire the leaders to commit through thick and thin.

And these unfortunate stories go on.

They may sound different, smell different, or look different, but they all come from the same shelf. Without the competent manager's skills on how to roll out change, initiatives, ministries, and programs, all come to naught.

It takes months of Sundays to gain the skills to lead and manage the church. It takes managerial competence, smarts, and savvy to plant and raise programs that grow tall as oaks from little acorns. It takes decades if you're figuring it out from the smoke of your breath. You certainly cannot do it by guess and by gosh.

That is why church builders need to act now, and they don't have the time for lengthy schooling.

Hence, this *Field Guide*.

It will give church builders like you the nuts and bolts on how to lead and manage in a way that brings out the best in church and coach you on the basics of how to hit the dusty and shifting ground running.

INCEPTION

This *Field Guide* is not the product of the speculative musings of a man with a graying beard. Nor is it the result of hard-core academic research, a dogged hunt for abstract intellections buried in books. We gathered the insights in this book from the soil and air of the lived experiences of many parish priests and lay leaders in the Philippines who—by the sweat of their brows—built stewardship churches that love and care for the poor.

As a backstory, Socio-Pastoral Institute (SPI) stumbled upon the spirituality of stewardship about 20 years ago, under the aegis of our mission partner St. Thomas More Parish in Denver, Colorado, USA. Upon recognizing the capacity of stewardship to transform people, communities, and churches, SPI adopted the whole enchilada. Stewardship has transformed our institution from top to bottom, outside in. As a result, we have been promoting it at full throttle around the Philippines and beyond ever since.

As the Executive Director of SPI, I am witness to the efforts of parish priests and lay leaders around the Philippines who introduced as-big-as-a-barn Stewardship Programs in their churches. We became the de facto harbor of the many conquests, triumphs, letdowns, and fiascos of the pioneers who adopted stewardship.

It is from this sanctuary that we gathered what works in building a stewardship church that loves the poor.

The foot in the door was to gather in one heap the varied experiences of the pioneer leaders who built stewardship churches in the Philippines. This big data is composed of almost two decades' worth of praxis that came from faraway churches in Infanta, San Pablo, Tuguegarao, Pangasinan, and Davao to nearby churches in Novaliches, Cubao, Cavite, and Manila.

We struggled to cut through the data noise in search of luster and illumination. We stood watchfully at the massive rolling, heaving, breathing information, like whalers on swift boats with harpoons ready to snag the elusive but extraordinary actions that worked.

While we quickly caught some of the best practices, some hid like thieves on the lam. Many refused to give up without a fight. Still, identifying these astonishing methods and insights was just the rough-and-ready beginnings. They were the low-lying fruits, ripe for the picking.

The trouble was that unless we catalog all the gathered gems into a systematic method, leadership and management of church renewal remained elusive as unicorns. Without a methodical process, it was all touch and go. Some of the best practices and principles came to us some days and nights; some left us some days and nights.

Such a gift was not a worthy offering to church builders.

Church builders deserve something solid, something they can sink their teeth into, and something that can chaperon them through the processes of inception, consolidation, expansion, and mainstreaming of stewardship and the Church of the Poor. Church builders deserve a *Field Guide* that's sure-footed but easy to digest, an instrument that doesn't read like a scientific journal or a technical manual.

Thus, the second and more grueling stage of the struggle is to wrap these best practices and insights inside a step-by-step process that, when followed, gives the leaders a leading edge to success.

This was the harder nut to crack.

The days passed in the hunt for this incremental procedure. It was a cunning and slippery beast that hid in the shadows; hence, we struggled to seize it and grab it by its forelocks. There were many dark times when we felt like little colored balls lost and abandoned in neck-high weeds. But we persevered and plodded along. We prayed for the tide to turn.

When the epiphany came, a heavy anchor was lifted from our necks. At last, the 7-Step procedure to build a stewardship church that loves the poor! This is, in our estimation, the paragon guide—the observed of all observers. It is not just a pretty pair of shoes for the journey; it is a glowing torch to help church builders navigate the dark and befuddling labyrinth of pastoral leadership and management for the graceful transformation of the church.

THE FOUR BATTLEGROUNDS

The venture to promote transformative change in the church, in contraposition to careless change that is here today but gone tomorrow, is a perplexing and difficult one. As things go, it involves jugglery—deftly keeping a few balls in the air.

The pioneer builders' experience reveals that to win the warfare, *they must wage a sustained campaign on four key battlegrounds.*

The Four Battlegrounds of Transformational Change

1. To shift the mission priorities of the church from caring for the *saved few* and *revenue*, to making disciples who care for humanity and the world.

2. To build and strengthen institutional programs, mechanisms, and processes that will ensure the success of this alternative church model.

3. To teach the congregation the disciple's habits of praying, serving, giving, and loving the poor.

4. To build a new culture that will set all the desired transformations in place.

The imperilment is that to fail in even one of them is to give up the war. This is why the road to success is gnarled and tangled, this is why so many of our leaders miss the boat.

Those who ignored one or two of the battlegrounds came apart at the seams. Some institutionalized and developed the Stewardship Program. But they did not make a dent in the renewal of the Lay Organizations, Movements, and Associations (LOMA); Parish Pastoral Council (PPC); and Worship, Education, Service, Temporalities, Youth, Family and Life (WESTY Fam) Ministries. (In this book, I will just refer to the various church ministries as "Ministries.") Some succeeded at increasing offertory giving. But they drew a blank at promoting volunteerism, prayer, and service to the poor. Some changed the congregations' habits on prayer, service, and giving. But, since they failed to shift the priorities of the church, the newfound resources were devoted to beautification efforts instead of making disciples. All the pastors who failed to change the culture saw their hard-earned efforts belly-up when they were eventually reassigned to other parishes.

To promote transformational change, we must address the Four Battleground concerns.

The modus operandi is as tough as old boots and as onerous to mull over. But don't worry, the 7-Step procedure has your back. It has the Four Battleground operations sewn up and in the bag. We will tackle the big-league endeavors one spoonful at a time so we don't bite off more than we can gnaw.

The trick is to **use stewardship as the foundation stone** of our struggle for long-lasting change and renewal. *We must employ stewardship like a falling domino tile to generate a chain reaction, a concatenation of events to win the day in all the Four Battlegrounds.*

Not to do so is to tilt at windmills.

TAKE WHAT YOU NEED

Regrettably, this 7-Step process is not idiotproof.

This is not the bell, book, and candle that will miraculously make everything right as rain. You cannot go through the motions and expect success. You need situational awareness, critical thinking, common sense, and creativity about yourself at all times. Remember, you are not making noodle soup (add egg, stir, and presto!). You are—for crying out loud—transforming the church!

Pay heed also that this 7-Step method is a guide, not the Ten Commandments carved in stone. You can break it and stray from it yet still remain sinless and without fault. This is not a binary all-or-nothing proposition either. Adopt what you think is useful and leave behind the rest.

In plain English, if the 7-Step prescription here runs counter to your experience and does not work in your situation, by all means, *deviate, experiment, innovate, explore.*

Dare to cut new trails always.

That said, we deem this guide solid and safe as houses. It is reliable as we braced it to the beam of the experiences of priests and lay leaders who built stewardship churches in the Philippines that love the poor. We believe this 7-Step procedure will work here and abroad. We think it's up the alley of the churches in the cities and megapolis, and churches in one-carabao barrios.

Aspiringly, this *Field Guide* will enable even novice church builders to confront the greatest dangers involved in church renewal with the greatest prudence.

On that account, we urge you to suck this lemon dry.

THE *7 STEPS* TO TRANSFORMATIONAL CHANGE

For you to try and tackle a host of concerns all at once is to spread yourself too thin. This is the prescription for disaster—no ifs, ands, or buts about it. To steer away from this imminent danger, I urge you to follow the proverb *duos insequens lepores, neutrum capit* (Erasmus's *Adagia*), which means "He who chases two hares catches neither."

That said, please go through these *7 Steps* sequentially.

Step 1. Sound the Alarm!

Step 2. Form Your Own Delta Force

Step 3. Figure Out the *Why, What & How* of Stewardship

Step 4. Launch Massive Stewardship Formation Campaigns

Step 5. Roll Out the Pledges

Step 6. Shift the Gravity of the Church to Favor the Poor

Step 7. Make Stewardship the Dominant Church Culture

Bring everything to bear on one thing at a time. Stick to that one thing until you get it right. Only then do you move on to the next concern. Focus is the key to achieving uncommon success.

How do you reach the summit of Mount Apo?

One step at a time.

How do you transform the church?

One step at a time.

OUR PRAYER

Come loaf with me.

Set aside an afternoon or two to read this book.

I invite you to swirl the ideas around in your mouth and tongue. Pay close attention to the rubbery and hard-to-chew details. Masticate. Take your sweet time. Savor the various notions until the tart, charred, briny, bittersweet, and tangy notes come together and make sense.

At a certain point, I urge you to swallow and digest.

When you get it, when you think you've nailed it down, please consider that the heart of the matter is not about what we know but about what we do. Knowledge is well and good, but it is our actions that define us.

It is our actions that change the world.

As it is our proclivity to sit on our hands, let us end this chapter by imploring the Lord to give us the courage and grit to start this quest and see it through.

May the good Lord bless and keep us.

May He blow the flickering embers in our bellies back to roaring life.

May He embolden us to set His house on fire!

Amen.

STEP 1: SOUND THE ALARM!

I HAVE YET TO MEET a person who, when asked to confront a crisis or adapt to evolving circumstances, said, "Great! Let's start now!"

The fact is, it is a rare bird who embraces change with passion and gets on top of it like an Argentinian tango dancer. For all and sundry, when the winds of change come calling, we bury our heads in the sand and pray for things to get better.

That's because we are small creatures who abhor change.

Our minds are so trapped to thinking "inside the box" that unconventional ideas and perspectives rarely come and visit. We love familiar things: We shackle ourselves like chattel slaves to our comfort zones, habits, and traditions. Our beloved mantra is the well-trodden path, come rain or shine!

To that extent, how do you then persuade people whose default compulsions are stasis and complacency to get aboard a bus headed to a destination unknown—an alternative way of being church?

This predicament is the first trial that a church builder faces. He must cross swords to subdue this disposition. If he cannot overwhelm it, he has but a dog's chance in building a stewardship church that loves the poor.

The opening salvo in this adventure, therefore, is for the parish priest to **sound the alarm**!

He must rock the boat and disconcert the hell out of everybody by proclaiming that the church is in crisis. He must repeatedly declare that we are in a predicament so dark that to do nothing is to be complicit in the church's dissolution.

This is how he can unsettle people who will gladly run a mile to stay rooted to the same spot, to do something.

No queue jumping here—this is an obligatory first step!

The church builder must communicate this concern to all key parish leaders. He ought to sit down shoulder to shoulder with his leaders and bring them around to this point of view. He should have a chat with his Parish Pastoral Council (PPC) and the heads of Lay Organizations, Movements, and Associations (LOMA) and Ministries.

If he cannot start face-to-face dialogues, he must organize encounters via Skype, Zoom, Google Meet, Microsoft Teams, or other apps that make virtual meetings possible.

After swaying the church's key leaders, opinion makers, and influencers, the parish priest must then cast a wider net. He must stop and talk with anybody who will listen and persuade them even by a bit that things are truly not up to scratch. He must steep his homilies with concern that the church is in dire straits.

The church builder must do this day in, day out with his hand on his heart and with gusto and conviction.

The point here is to create a sense of urgency that will wash the people clean of their aversion to change. The goal is to prepare God's people to pull the trigger.

Bear in mind, we will only haul buckets of water if there is a conflagration that threatens to reduce everything we hold dear to ashes. Under any other condition, we would rather malinger and while away the hours watching the latest viral videos on TikTok and YouTube.

To put it bluntly, to not sound the alarm bells is to have a snowball's chance in hell to rouse people off their tails.

It's like showing up with a knife in a gunfight to the death.

THE FOUR BATTLEGROUNDS

This chapter is about

✓ **Reframing the priorities of the church toward making disciples**. (Take note that this battleground is a crucial first step among the four battle areas we must win to revivify the church.)

The other battlegrounds are

- Changing the habits of the congregation
- Strengthening church programs and mechanisms
- Promoting a new culture that will crystallize and solidify the changes

BAROMETER OF HEALTH

But is the church in a crisis? Or is the crisis a conjured ghost, an apparatus made up by church builders to trick the people to throw the great cast?

Let's take a minute and examine how to determine the state of the church by reflecting on these queries: What is the state of the church today? Is she in fine fettle or big trouble? How did things ever get this far?

Without a standard way of obtaining an accurate measure of the church, trying to read her well-being is like trying to read tea leaves or the wind. Do we leave the church alone, as everything is top-notch? Or do we administer cardiopulmonary resuscitation, as she is on her last legs?

Given the wealth of diagnoses and views that are all over the shop, we could not say for sure.

Some suggest that the true valuation of the church is by the quality and state of her building and facilities; others claim it is all about the pastor's noteworthiness and character; many declare it is by the number of warm bodies that pack the Sunday services; while one or two insist it is all about the wealth of social, medical, and material services she offers to the poverty-stricken.

Children and fools beg to disagree.

They say that there is only one barometer that can reveal if the church is in good form or not. And this is by how well she realizes her original purpose: *Her mission.*

This yardstick is the only surefire way to tell apart churches that fetch water from churches that float like perished leaves on the river. This is the unimpaired touchstone that reveals if the church will live another thousand years or if she is but a hop, skip, and a jump away from obsolescence and extinction.

Not to mince words, if the church is locked to the mission 24/7, then the church is hale and hearty. If the church dillydallies with the mission, then the church is withered in the vine.

To lay it out clearly, the mission is not just one of the Catholic Church's many concerns—it is its only concern. The mission is not one of the many ambitions of the church—it is its only ambition. It is the rhyme and reason of who we are; it is the rhyme and reason of what we do.

The mission is the whole kit and caboodle!

But what is the mission of the church?

If you couldn't make head or tail of it, let's clap eyes on God's Word about the *Great Commission.*

"Go therefore and make disciples of all nations, baptizing them in the name of the Father and of the Son and of the Holy Spirit, teaching them to observe all that I have commanded you; and lo, I am with you always, to the close of the age." (Matthew 28:19–20)

MAKING DISCIPLES

There it is!

Our appointment is to make disciples. This is our purpose, our why, our wherefore. This is the singular task we must discharge well if we are to flourish like a mango tree by a flowing stream.

If the church's calling is to make disciples, we must investigate and think through two complexities in order to fulfill it:

1. What makes a disciple a disciple?

2. How do you make one?

I will answer the first question here and contend with the second in another chapter. Let's dive right in!

A brief answer is that **a disciple is a follower of Jesus, one who is committed to Jesus *and* his mission.**

The first portion of that definition—steadfastness to the person of Jesus—has the earmarks of simplicity and easy intelligibility. Let's leave that well alone and move on.

It is the second detail—adherence to the mission of Jesus—that makes us stumble. If we are uncertain what Jesus's mission is, then we are doomed to fail. **How can we be a follower of Jesus if we do not know or cannot commit to what He dedicated his life to?** That is the humdinger! Let us run Christ's mission again:

"The Spirit of the Lord is upon me, because he has anointed me to preach good news to the poor. He has sent me to proclaim release to the captives and recovering of sight to the blind, to set at liberty those who are oppressed, to proclaim the acceptable year of the Lord." (Luke 4:18–19)

Jesus came to save the world. He dedicated his entire life to this purpose. And this is also why he suffered and died on the cross.

The hard nut to crack is the nature of the salvation Jesus brings.

This is called by many names: a new heaven and a new earth, the kingdom of God, the reign of God, and the Good News. The terms look and sound different, but they are of the same blood. They all refer to total salvation or the redemption of both body and soul.

This sweeping salvation has two enactments. In the second coming's culmination and fullness, God will liberate us from sickness, pain, suffering, and death. He will walk among us in this *new heaven and new earth.*

In the meantime, the kingdom has a provisional, imperfect manifestation that is often described as "here but not yet." This passing embodiment of God's reign is often imaged as *a new world order marked by justice, peace, and integrity of creation.* The PCP II document delineates it as a "civilization of life and love" (no. 255).

My turn of mind is to describe this temporal salvation as a world filled with good stewards who take care of one another and all creation.

In view of this, what kind of disciples or Jesus-followers should the church produce?

- Unwavering people who are committed to Jesus's mission of total salvation
- Industrious folks whose lifework is to uplift the poor, free the captives, heal the sick, liberate the oppressed, and heal the land
- Good stewards who care for humankind and all creation

LOSING OUR WAY

If making disciples is the raison d'être—the most important and central justification for the church—you would presuppose that all the church programs, ministries, projects, staff, and activities are measured and evaluated against this flag.

But you would be wrong.

Many churches do not evaluate and calibrate their performance according to the mission. For this reason, we find most churches wanting when stacked up against the big "What for?"

If churches gallop away from making disciples, what do they employ as the substitute goal post of success?

By the sniff of my nose, it's this: To ensure that they pack the church on Sundays and that the financial donations are enough to cover the operating expenses. Meeting the twin goals of "revenue" and "serving the core," many declare these churches to have the world by the tail.

In this contrivance, "revenue" and "care for the saved few" equal victories and unimpeachable justification for the house of God. They see making disciples—ministering to the "lost sheep," the poor, the sick, the marginalized, the exploited, and lapsed Catholics—as optional rather than an indispensable dimension of the church.

Before the coronavirus pandemic, most parish priests in the big cities met these substitute institutional goals effortlessly.

Why do I say that?

How hard could it be when 80 percent of the 111 million Filipinos are Catholic? Surely, the parish priest could gather a thousand or two among the fifty thousand of his parishioners who will go to Sunday mass? Surely, the parish priest could find a few hundred among the fifty thousand of his parishioners who will donate money to meet operating costs?

If the parish priests in the big cities with oodles of parishioners couldn't even do that in the time before the pandemic, then we are doomed!

It is worthy to note that the two spurious goals of "revenue" and "ministering to the saved" are, in actuality, two sides of the same coin. They are joined at the hip because if one worships on the altar of riches, it makes a ton of commercial sense to target existing customers or the committed core of parishioners who go to church every Sunday. And it is, likewise, prudent not to lift a finger on behalf of the "lost sheep."

Why?

Because 80 percent of profits come from 20 percent of one's current customers. That is a truism in business held dear by all for-profit corporations and enterprises. The regular Mass-goers are the money-spinners. Time after time, they come through to sweeten the kitty and fill up the coffers. Without them, the house of worship will be beggared and fall to hard times. Not for nothing are they well looked-after and cared-for by the church.

Making disciples or developing new "customers" entails shelling out wads of money. Based on the experience of corporations, it costs five times more to bring in a new customer than to hold fast to old ones. Disturbingly, that is the reason many of our churches turn a blind eye to the unchurched.

The naked fact is, if your bottom line is the bottom line, it is as simple as it can be: It makes all the sense in the world to concentrate on your core. It does not wash to spend and throw away money on the "lost sheep."

And that's the fly in the ointment.

What about making disciples of all nations? How can we see that winged assignment through when we don't even take care of the least, the last, and the lost *in our own parishes*?

EVALUATION: A DANCE OF TWO STEPS

How did things get so bad? How did the church drift away from making disciples?

To unravel this ball of wax, we have to comprehend the significance of the church services housed under the roofs of the ministries and programs, like worship, community organizing, formation, outreach, music, and counseling.

It is through these services that we make disciples.

If we find the ministries and programs wanting, then the church falls flat on its face and fails in her mission. But if they live up to expectations, then the church delivers the goods. This is how vital the programs and ministries are—they are at the frontline, at the very coalface of the mission.

Now, what is the general state of our ministries and programs?

Even with a furtive glance, we find that many churches don't even bother to keep their program and ministry bats straight. The primary culprit for this botched situation is that they do not evaluate their programs, ministries, activities, and personnel.

Why is it crucial that all churches hardwire the regular conduct of evaluating their systems and programs?

Because evaluation is the lightning crack that makes people, programs, and ministries better. It is the jolt that ensures that everything we do is *for the mission.* By revealing where the shoe pinches and where it fits, evaluations show us what is going well and what needs more work—critical insights to tweaking the programs and ministries so that they hum and operate according to plan. When we weigh performance against outcomes, we learn how far along we've actually gone in getting the deed done.

Expressly, evaluation is the secret sauce of institutional development and church renewal. It is a godsend that brings a sight of helpful treats. Unfortunately, many church leaders do not recognize the importance of evaluations. Or they are unaware of what the evaluation process brings to the reanimation of the church. For this reason, pastors and lay leaders often run the ministries and programs by feel, experience, intuition, inspiration, and common sense unburdened by the insights and recommendations from evaluations.

Many are allergic to what they call the corporate method that leans on *logical frames* and the *planning, implementation, monitoring, and evaluation cycle.* They favor the spontaneous management style of playing it by ear and flying by the seat of their pants—a surefire way to dull the sharp blade of the mission.

In its simplest terms, evaluation is a dance of two steps. Most clinkers happen because leaders take the convenient shortcut and do away with the second step of this already sparse dance routine.

Dance Step #1

The opening gambit is to **determine if the services and programs achieved their purposes**. At its nub are five basic questions:

1. What is the program's aim?
2. What happened?
3. What went well and why?
4. What went wrong and why?

5. What do we do now?

Dance Step #2

The next move is to **examine how the services and programs contributed to the overall institutional goal of making disciples**.

If that is as clear as mud, let's gather it all in one handful and consider how it applies to a children's bible study program.

The goal of the children's bible study program is to help children get the picture and make sense of the word of God. The first step in the evaluation process, therefore, is to find out if the program achieved what it had set out to do. Did the children come away with more knowledge and understanding of the Scriptures? Did they get the point?

The next step is to find out if the children became disciples. Was there a positive change in the children's patterns of behaviors after the course? Are they now exhibiting an increase in good thoughts, words, and deeds?

Pay heed that the purpose of the bible study is not only to increase the children's knowledge and comprehension of the bible but also **to *transform* the children so that they become disciples**. To focus on program actions and outputs (e.g., perfect attendance, kids exhibiting high to perfect bible verse recall) is to miss the forest from the trees; it is to abandon the ultimate target outcome of making disciples for brownie points on technical excellence.

When you look to see which way the wind blows, you'll find that most churches fall to pieces here. It is not their second nature to calibrate their programs and activities to disciple-making.

So how do these wayward churches determine if they are successful or not?

Without an eye on evangelization, the common run is for churches to designate busyness as the key determinant and indicator of program success. In this mad algebra, activity equals success: The busier their ministries and programs, the more the parishioners rate them as five-star; the more actions the LOMA and Ministries carry out, the more the people see the church as a howling success.

In this train of thought, the objective of ministries and programs is to make a boatload of happenings and activities. Some activities may be pointless, like pounding salt or counting beans. But so long as the church is busy and running nowhere fast, we appraise them as examples worth emulating.

No wonder the church is grasping at straws.

WIDESPREAD MALAISE

The sad effect of the mission being relinquished is, after a while, most of the faithful become comfortably numb and learn to go along with this errant stream.

Like small birds in nests, we soon agree that the church is—and will always remain—a haven for the "saved," the choir boys, and the kindly matrons. We rationalize that if we include the multitude of the poverty-stricken and excluded, there will not be enough room in the church to swing a cat. We lull ourselves to sleep that it is okay for the church to devote 90 percent of her time and resources to care for the one sheep who is already in a safe place.

From there, we are but a nudge away from sweeping the other *99 lost sheep* under the rug. **We turn the parable of the Good Shepherd on its head to convince ourselves that to** *lose 99 sheep but save 1* **is good enough.**

The propensity to settle for good enough is how we lost our way. We went after small beers and loose change, such as occasional acts of charity, beautification drives, and a few street masses here and there. Woefully, we abandoned the precious gold in the ground that can only be mined through leadership development, lay empowerment, social action, formation, and community organizing.

It doesn't make horse sense, but we sadly made it happen. Why?

Because excellence in mission—like mining for gold—is back-breaking work. We dream of victory but refuse to go through the mill; we yearn for pearls but refuse to dive into the deep.

Small wonder we went for the low-lying fruits, for the cheap coins on the footway.

That is how we let the mission slip through our fingers.

THE GREAT OMISSION

Everything springs from and comes back to making disciples. Mission alone flows outward and inward and completes itself. Whatever is said and done returns to the mission. Everything else will go by the board.

The church lives, thrives, or dies depending on the caliber of the disciples we make.

Will the disciples stick to the mission as white sticks to rice? Will they put their heads on the block for God and others? Or will they suck out our church's air and resources and leave none for the rest of us?

Make no bones about it, we are in an unprecedented crisis because we're awful at making disciples. None is so blind as those who won't see that the crisis of the church is about failure in making disciples. None is so deaf as those who won't hear that we need to be better at making disciples.

This is the crisis whose roots we should hack at a thousandfold. This is the catastrophe that our leaders must overcome.

This is the rot in the church that we must subdue and smash to smithereens.

WHAT NOW?

Allow me to pivot and end this chapter on a positive note.

The comforting prospect is that once we become fully aware of the crisis, we can never unsee or unknow it. Crisis gives us a profound realization of what is crucial against what is mundane and a waste of time. Crisis leaves an enduring perspective, a lasting viewpoint we carry with us to our last days.

The question is: Will we act on this newfound perspective or not?

We can wave a dead chicken at the crisis in the hopes it will go away. Or we can put our hands to the plow and address our collective failure in making disciples. If you choose to roll up your sleeves, the first step to the reanimation of the church is to do a deep dive into what we mean by a disciple and how we make one.

This is where the Stewardship Program checks in and joins the dance.

TAKEAWAYS

The first step in building a stewardship church is to **sound the alarm to predispose people to action**.

What Is Our Core Message?

The church is in a crisis: We are failing in our mission to make disciples who will care for all of humanity and all creation.

Auxiliary Messages on the Roots of the Crisis?

- We strayed from the mission of making disciples and focused on revenue and the saved.
- We do not evaluate programs and performance against the church's mission.
- We equated program success with busyness.
- We became complacent.

Action Points

1. Engage the PPC, LOMA, and Ministries' leaders. Convince them to address this crisis. Focus on the crisis, not on the solutions.

2. If you cannot have face-to-face encounters with your leaders, have virtual meetings and remote learning using

video conferencing apps, like Skype, Zoom, Google Meet, or Microsoft Teams.

3. Sound the alarm in your homilies.

4. Talk to anyone who will listen and encourage people to talk about the crisis.

STEP 2: BUILD A DELTA FORCE TEAM

WILL THE CHURCH TRAVERSE great distances, meander around the lives of peoples throughout the land, and bring sweet blessings to one and all? Or will it trip up in sandy beds, turn to dust, and fall short of its avowed goals, purposes, and mission?

The pastor is the flowing water that cuts the soil and forms the gullies which turn into the living rivers that are our churches and our communities. As the parish head, he can steer the church this way or that, thus or so. He can bend the church by his will. He can paraphrase the church according to his abilities, recondition it according to his passions and transmute it according to his inclinations and predispositions.

If he is a terrible overseer, he can send the church into a disastrous tailspin. If he is a consummate leader, he can raise the church to new heights and make it flourish—like wildflowers in the field.

This is an oppressive load and responsibility for any man to carry. Unfortunately, this is the burden that all parish priests must bear, and it is grossly unfair.

But that's how the ball bounces in the church.

How a leader makes and carries out decisions is at the heart of what we call leadership style. From the top of my head, the dominant practice in the church seems to alternate between the directive and consultative styles. Using this strange brew, the pastor, on some days, relies only on himself to make and implement decisions; on other days, he solicits help and inputs from key church leaders.

What style he employs for which situation seems to be without rhyme or reason. Perhaps it is even unknown to the priest himself! I call this leadership style *to-ing* and *fro-ing*.

Since leadership style is crucial to the church's well-being, some consider it a hanging matter to leave it to the pastor's whims and fancies to determine how to govern. Others hesitate to dive into the thick of this question. They tiptoe around this touchy issue because they believe it is the absolute prerogative of the pastor to lead how he chooses—regardless of its consequences to the church and her parishioners.

The early adopters of stewardship churches that love the poor, however, have something definite to say on this.

It is their experience that **the parish priests who made the grade were the ones who shared their leadership and managerial responsibilities with teams.** By going full hog with their teams and activating co-thinking and co-doing, the pastors empowered their lay to build this new church with them. Likewise, by bouncing ideas off one another and working cohesively to get things done, the teams made this herculean work lighter and the impossible possible.

To the pioneers, this issue about leadership style is moot and academic. Assuming you want a church that lives up to expectations—a church that delivers the goods—then the pastor must adopt the philosophy, processes, and mechanisms of consultative-participative leadership. He must go all-in with teams and teamwork because *collaboration and partnerships are the linchpins of success.*

For the pastor to do otherwise is to meet with disaster.

To the pioneers, this is as clear as day.

FORMING THE DELTA TEAM

When the high command of the United States Army wants something done and done well, they send in their tier one, special mission unit to do the trick: The Delta Force. It makes all the sense in the world to send your crack-team to carry out the toughest assignments. If you send your second-stringers, you flirt with the mission going to rack and ruin.

This brings us to the second step on how to make a stewardship church that loves the poor: **Establish your own Delta Team.**

Led by the parish priest, this team is the tip of the spear in the struggle for church renewal. It serves as the priest's right arm that decides on matters of great import and puts them in effect. Boiled down to its fundamentals, this team oversees the birthing of a peculiar church—the stewardship church that loves the poor.

In the parish's situation, the Parish Pastoral Council (PPC) is on the leading edge in running the church. It is, therefore, the natural unit to play the white knight in our push to build this stewardship church. The only caveat is, there are often PPC members who are not genuine church leaders. These members came to their positions by their professional accomplishments, age, gender, length of service to the church, or personal connections to the hierarchy. Unless you want to see your hard work go to waste, you don't want leaders who are not sharp as tacks in your elite team.

That said, it is gainful for you to create a new group—your own Delta Force. By doing so, you start with a fresh canvas that you can populate with leaders who will get the job done and done well!

What you call this elite team is not important.

You can call this group Stewardship Team; Renewal Team; Not Fast, Just Furious Team; or whatever seems apt and meaningful. The point is, by not using the PPC, you don't paint yourself into a corner where you're forced to work with leaders worth a row of pins. While most of your Delta Force candidates will come from the PPC, you might find one or two diamonds in the rough elsewhere in the parish.

Team Composition

Regarding the Delta Force's composition, **you need a mix of**

People Connectors, Opinion Influencers, Thinkers, and Doers. Without People Connectors, reaching out to gather the multitudes will be a tall order. Without Influencers, winning people over to your side and cause will be an upstream swim. Without Thinkers, you won't be able to do a course correction, and you will lose your way. Without Doers, all your dreams will remain castles in the air.

As most church leaders are of advanced age, you must choose those who still have something left in the gas tank. Remember, this undertaking is not a walk in the park. It is, in reality, a grueling marathon that demands the utmost stamina and determination. Consequently, to inhabit the Delta Team with leaders on their last legs is to come to a pretty pass.

Equally vital is to pick people with high emotional intelligence. This means you should do your best to fill your Team with leaders who manage their emotions as well as handle their interpersonal relationships judiciously and gracefully. All it takes is a lone leader who is insensitive, tactless, and indifferent to scare many of your prospects away from the Delta Team. A sharp tongue is like a keen knife that can cut and draw blood. In contrast, a sympathetic leader who plucks up people's courage and lifts their spirits can rally the Team to third base in no time.

Variety is another thing to consider in tacking a team together. Aim for a mixed-skills, mixed-traits Delta Team. Tap the leaders who have unique talents, cultural experiences, and skill-sets that you need. **More important, recruit people who vary in educational and professional accomplishments and come from different socioeconomic levels.**

It often takes new perspectives, fresh techniques, and new thinking to solve stubborn, chronic problems that have plagued the church for ages. Whenever a group of people with diverse knowledge, backgrounds, skills, and know-how talk problems out and brainstorm potential solutions, it often leads to outside-the-box thinking and breakthroughs.

Team Size

Regarding the Delta Team's size, the key is to keep it to a number that is easy to wield. If you have too many members, some leaders will slack off and free ride on other members' creativity and energy. If the Team is too small, you might not have the broad-based skills you need to take the church in new and exciting directions. The small size might also push members to wear too many hats and burn the candle at both ends.

The rule of thumb, according to our pioneers' experience, is to **start with 15 prospects**.

But why begin with a bagful of candidates?

Many prospects are overwhelmed when they learn about the mission to renew the church and what the Delta Force requires from them. So, faster than fast, they fall like trees and are never seen again. It is therefore prudent to ramp up the number right off the bat. This way, you have some wiggle room in case some candidates opt out of the Team midstream.

When forming the Team, the key is to engage with the candidates and have one-on-one sit-downs. This is your chance to pitch it strong but never pitch it false. Be honest and forthcoming. Do not lead them down the primrose path. Let them know exactly what they are joining.

State the problem: **The church is in crisis because church leaders forgot to prioritize the Mission.**

Explain the Delta Team's purpose: **They are the lead unit that will address this crisis and bring about church renewal.**

Make your prospects aware that this involves building an alternative church model—a stewardship church that loves the poor. Come right out and say that it could take years of pounding away to achieve this dream. Above all, let them know that you cannot do this without a Delta Force beside you going at it tooth and nail.

Make it plain why you are inviting them, what traits or qualities they have that make them a good fit for the Delta Force. Explain what membership to the Team will require from them—two afternoons a month for Delta Force meetings and five afternoons a month for actual church and community work. It is only after they have ticked all the boxes that you ask if they can commit to this Team.

Once over this hurdle of securing your prospects' commitment, you can now organize the first Delta Force meeting.

Think of this first formal meeting as something like "Flashback Friday." But instead of reposting your old photos and memories on Facebook, you revisit with the group so that they can undergo the process together as one unit. Repeat to them what you have discussed in your one-on-one sit-downs.

Because you have secured the commitment of your prospects beforehand, with any luck, there won't be any unpleasant surprises in the orientation.

So lather, rinse, and repeat.

Tell them again how the church is in a crisis because she is not making disciples. Show that to address the crisis, we need to build a stewardship church that loves the poor. Underline with a big black marker that it may take many years to pull it off. Let them know you need a Delta Force, that you cannot do this by yourself. Ask if they can set aside seven afternoons a month for this high-priority endeavor.

Before you wrap up, ask everyone in the Team to speak up and share their sentiments and viewpoints about this new mission. Then end with a prayer, and ask the Lord to accompany this newly minted Delta Force to victory.

THE FOUR BATTLEGROUNDS

This chapter is about
- ✓ **Creating new institutional mechanisms to promote transformational change**

The other three are
- Resetting the priorities of the church
- Changing the habits of God's people

- Putting up a new culture that will make the changes permanent

THE POWER OF TEAMS

Why is putting teams into action the only way to make the grade in this journey to a church renewed?

This is because of the simple certainty that *no one* **of us is better than** *all of us*. It doesn't matter how exceptional you are. If you're playing solo—if you're pushing, pulling, and heaving by yourself—you will always lose to a team.

Here is the extravagant arithmetic of collectives, groups, and aggregates: Many are better than one, whole integers exceed fractions, a team of average people is superior to the lone genius. *Something magical happens when people of varying skills and assets come together to work toward a common purpose and goal.* They can overcome individual limitations and go to a place none of them could reach if they went there by themselves.

If you believe you are better than all your leaders working together, you are either a once-in-a-generation prodigy or guilty of the sin that felled the angels.

Fancy that!

Not a single church that rolled out stewardship managed successfully without a hardworking Delta Team behind it. No lone priest could have done it on his own. He needed the Team's range of experience, expertise, and hands to move the church forward.

Without a team behind him, even the worthiest priest plays himself out.

There are good things to say about financial and human resources, high technology, knowledge, and organizational systems. But teams have always been, and will always be, the top ingredient in the successful realization of institutional dreams, goals, and visions. **Teamwork is the supereminent way to make the church better—it is the engine for church renewal.**

With teamwork, we will reach distant shores. Without it, we will soon scud heavy gales under bare poles.

That is why the pastor must be on the pin with his Delta Force.

That is why he must buckle down to ensure this Team's success.

THE CLUMSY ELEPHANT

Let us now talk about the clumsy elephant in the room, the nemesis that diminishes the power of teams—groupthink. Groupthink is the propensity of individual group members to go along for the sake of getting along.

We are herd animals hardwired to go with the flow, so we conform to the opinions and decisions of the group. For this reason, many individuals who are opposed to the group's ideas or decisions choose to keep silent and set aside their opinions rather than ruffle feathers.

Groupthink is felt and most prevalent in strappingly hierarchical organizations like the military and the church. In these organizations, there is palpable fear that the group might censure the men and women at the bottom of the totem pole for not going with the tide.

Many priests choose to keep silent rather than go against even the misguided opinions and decisions of their bishop. The laity will bite their lips rather than contradict even the mistaken opinions of their parish priest. Rank-and-file members of Lay Organizations, Movements, and Associations (LOMA) and Ministries will not utter a word against even the foolish sentiments and thoughts of their lay leaders.

And so it goes.

By putting a lid on the contrary ideas and perspectives bubbling from below, groupthink short-circuits the power of teams and shuts it down. It upsets the give-and-take, learn-from-each-other group dynamics and turns it all into a pile of manure—a perfect breeding ground for autocracies and dictatorships.

It is not uncommon to find parishes, LOMA, and Ministries run by leaders who ignore the creative interventions and inputs from their followers. They treat members like nincompoops and blatherskites who are incapable of coherent thought, fresh ideas, or inspiration. They value their members for their grunt work. Yet no one says a word about how this kills the teams' morale and effectiveness. Everyone is as quiet as a grave.

Everyone prefers not to rock the boat nor ruffle any feathers.

To not deal with groupthink defeats the rationale of building a Delta Force. Why surround yourself with capable people if you will not use their intelligence and talents? It's like keeping huge, ferocious guard dogs and barking yourself.

As awful as this may be to the rank and file, authoritarianism also corrupts the leaders themselves. Even a modest, levelheaded person, when given a blank check to run an institution anyway he wants—bereft of checks and balances, without performance reviews and evaluations—soon thinks of himself as better than all the rest.

At some point, he turns into a legend in his mind.

To cement his standing and position, he does away with inquiries and evaluations that could reveal the cupboards as bare. He empowers and surrounds himself with sycophants—yes-men who do not challenge him, point to the error of his ways, or bring him the bad news. Because no one tells him his mistakes and weaknesses, the authoritarian leader inhabits a strange world divorced from reality—a world where he is the penultimate commander, without blemish or fault.

Ignorant of what is happening, unable to tell what is right from wrong, incapable of separating reality from delusion, the leader fights a losing battle to keep the institution upright and on course. When a crisis appears on the horizon, the autocratic leader cannot change course to avoid it. He cannot rely on others around him for fresh, bold ideas to deal with the impending danger since he surrounds himself with people whose dominant traits are flattery and loyalty, not forthrightness and competence.

The story often ends badly. It concludes with the captain not only going down with his ship but the entire ship going down with the captain.

Holy smokes!

Alas, this is not a fairy tale. This is not about the happenings in a kingdom far, far away. **It is a story about *our time* and *our church***. A quick scout around shows that our dominant church archetype is one where the priest is the only person in a community of thousands who is gifted and capable. We deem the rest second-class citizens who are there to pay, pray, and obey.

In this model, there is only one eloquent mouth in the church; the rest are but ears whose ordained purpose is to follow the mouth. In this type of church, there is only one mind capable of serving a perpetual feast of ideas; the rest are but dumb hands valuable only for their menial, low-skilled, unpaid labor.

Thanks to groupthink, no one dare say a word about how this arrangement robs the church of its diverse brainpower and expertise. We are all as quiet as a mouse.

Not by chance are we all much poorer for it.

A pastor might have a great idea or plan for the church, but without the benefit of elaboration, correction, countersuggestion, or advice from others, the quality of his works will rarely reach its fullest potential.

If you have lay leaders around you who correct you, challenge your ideas, and offer alternative points of view, *consider them your greatest treasures and keep them close to your side*. They might hold your feet to the fire, get in your hair, and drive you up the wall. But they will make you a better pastor and a better person.

Let's put that in a pipe and smoke it for a few moments.

THE DELTA FORCE CULTURE

If groupthink is the team's cancer, what can we do to overcome it?

How do we turn this ragtag Delta Team into a force of nature?

To vanquish groupthink and nourish the power of teamwork, the parish priest should build and promote the cultures of collaboration and learning by trial and error.

What follows is a list of tips I gathered from the best practices of our stewardship pioneers.

Promote the Culture of Collaboration

- *Conduct Meetings as Roundtables*

  In this setup, everyone is of equal rank, and everyone can freely express an opinion or viewpoint without fear of censure or ridicule. The most influential people in the Team, like the parish priest and the head of the pastoral council, speak only after all the Team members have revealed their perspectives, thoughts, stance, judgment, and suggestions on the matters at hand.

  This maneuver is a surefire way to prevent team members from free-riding on the views and thoughts of the most influential leaders. It forces the unfocused to examine, postulate, speculate, and presuppose for themselves. It forces them to dig deep and look for original thoughts or opinions.

  Another ground rule in roundtable meetings is that *everyone must speak up.*

  This is to nudge even the most taciturn, unassertive, and mousiest team members to develop their powers of articulation so they can throw their two cents' worth in the ring. When everyone is engaged and rowing their oars, the uncommon benefit eventually comes to the Team.

- *Encourage Wild Ideas and Divergent Thinking*

  In brainstorming sessions, encourage everyone to propose potential solutions on the matter at hand. Write all the proffered suggestions and ideas on the whiteboard, including the far-out and bizarre. Ask the Team not to dismiss anything straightaway if the ideas appear wacko and beyond the pale at

first glance. Let the screwball propositions and wild suggestions sit and simmer before you ask the group to come to grips
with them.

This is a top priority because *we need divergent thinking to
overcome the chronic problems that have tormented the church
from all its born days.* Reliance on "tried and true" ideas and
"more of the same" thinking will not bring the leaps forward
and home runs we need.

- *Spur the Team to Build on Each Other's Ideas*

It is not everybody who can manufacture and unsheathe
groundbreaking ideas. Very few among us are mahatmas or
brainiacs who can cobble together original concepts at the
drop of a hat. Every man jack, on the other hand, can build
on, touch up, or sharpen somebody else's proposed solution or
course of action.

Therefore, to get the maximum creativity from the group,
*encourage all members to critique, improve, or support everybody
else's ideas, perspectives, judgments, and suggestions.* This is how
you bring your Delta Team in the zone—the state of exceptional focus where they are occupied with the business at
hand.

Promote Learning by Trial and Error

- *Fail Often to Succeed Shortly*

Trial and error trumps genius all the time.

It is the best game plan to realize even the loftiest of institutional goals and ambitions. In this paradigm, we regard
failure as the stepping stone to success. *We see failure as a fore-
ordained scourge in our lives as well as a valuable teacher who can
inculcate the fundamental insights we need to succeed.*

When the focus is on learning and not on victory-no-
matter-what and success-at-every-venture, the Delta Force is
emboldened to take more risks and tread uncertain paths to
realize biggish aspirations. They stick out their necks because

when they fail (yes, they *will* fail), no one will shame them for it or hold it against them. As it happens, the comprehension fortifies them that, in every miss, they learn something new and are thus one step closer to nailing it.

- **Encourage Research**

  In the hunt for a remedy to a problem, exhort everyone in the Delta Force to do basic research. Ask them all to enlarge their perspective and not rely on their stock knowledge, staple assumptions, or worn-out insights to find the solution to the point of issue. Request them to consult with the various stakeholders like religious groups, the unchurched, and small Christian communities. *They should pick the brains and seek the opinions of those most affected by the problem at hand.*

  Under this research-first or consult-the-people scheme, the Delta Force includes the larger community in dealing with impending issues. This improves the Team's chances of making the right decision that brings paramount benefits to the affected.

  It also ensures that implementation will proceed without major disruptions and pushback.

- **Employ the Pilot Approach**

  It is helpful to first try out your novel ideas and interventions on a small scale before you roll it out full-bore to the church at large. In this way, *you minimize the costs, risks, and disruptions while you gain invaluable real-world experience on implementation.*

  From this circumscribed involvement, you can get some insights on how to improve your plans, tweak staff capabilities, and adjust logistics. So when you roll out the program to the entire parish, you have already redone, reworked, and amended it for the better.

WHAT NOW?

Now that you have your Delta Force and running it in a way that inspires collaboration and learning, what's the first task that this Team must home in on?

Putting up the Stewardship Program!

And that is where we will jump to with both feet in the next chapter.

TAKEAWAYS

The second step in building a stewardship church that loves the poor is to **form your own Delta Force**.

Why Form a Delta Force?

To lead the charge in the church's renewal so that she lives up to her mission to make disciples.

The Team Composition:

- 15 initial candidates
- Assemble people who are Doers, Thinkers, People Connectors, and Influencers
- Find a mix of people who come from different socioeconomic backgrounds, have varied educational and professional accomplishments, and have diverse experiences, skills, and talents
- Look for leaders with time, ones who can commit seven afternoons a month: two for meetings, five for community actions
- Leaders with physical stamina
- Leaders with high emotional intelligence

How to Recruit?

Sit down with prospects one-on-one and give them the complete lay of the land: Tell them why you are forming the Delta Team, what the Team will do, why they were chosen, and what this undertaking requires of them.

How to Inaugurate the Delta Team?

Conduct an orientation meeting with all the candidates. Repeat the orientation you gave to the candidates in your one-on-one sessions. Ask them to commit to this endeavor. Bless the Team.

Establish a Group Culture that Celebrates

1. Collaboration

- Conduct all meetings as roundtables
- Encourage divergent thinking
- Spur team members to build on one another's ideas

2. Learning by trial and error

- Fail often to succeed quickly
- Encourage research
- Employ the Pilot approach

STEP 3: FIGURE OUT THE WHY, WHAT & HOW OF STEWARDSHIP

WE ARE DELICATE BEINGS in need of regular spiritual sustenance to scrape up the wherewithal so we could go through life unbowed and undiminished. I get my chosen fix from the sapient insights of extraordinary people. Here is an example of a paraphrased nutriment from the Buddha:

We make all created things twice—first, by mental conceptualization and then through the act of physical creation.

From this pronouncement, we can surmise that if the thought is unexamined and unrefined, the created occurrence is ambiguous and begrimed; if the thought is clear and well directed, the generated matter is straightforward and lucid.

It is crucial to take this insight to heart when building a stewardship church, for what is the Stewardship Program but a coarsened thought, an idea made concrete? As day follows night, if the stewardship proposition is incomprehensible and clouded, the Stewardship Program is rambling and ineffective. If the visualization of stewardship is sharp and right on the button, the created Stewardship Program is crisp and efficacious.

It is the height of hubris, therefore, to suppose that one can build the Stewardship Program by sheer luck or accident, without forethought and reflection. You cannot write a masterpiece with the slip of a pen. You cannot deliver a good homily by the slip of the tongue. You cannot build a stewardship church that loves the poor by the slip of the hand.

Moreover, it is foolish to suppose that one can build the Stewardship Program overnight. The farmer doesn't plant today and harvest tomorrow. To enjoy the bounty of the land, he must prepare the soil, sow and water the seed, and then regularly protect the sprout from rapacious birds and insects. It is only with delicate and superior effort over the gathering of many long days that the farmer secures and enjoys the blessings of the field.

This underlines the uncompromising actuality that **the rising to a worthwhile place is best undertaken deliberately, and the only way to the top is by the long, winding stairs of preparation, preparation, preparation**.

Yet many parish priests choose to introduce Stewardship Programs in their parishes without girding up their loins and figuring out the chief points and cold details in advance. They sally forth without a clear mental roadmap to escort them to where they want to go. Some are even uncertain why they embark on the stewardship journey. Following these largish oversights and bobbles, many ensnare their churches in nightmarish predicaments from which they cannot awaken.

THE WINDS OF CHANGE

Before sowing the first seeds of the Stewardship Program, it is prudent to mull over the substantial perturbations this will bring to the parish.

Rolling stewardship out will involve displacing a boatload of beloved traditions, norms, and long-held practices. It will mean inducing the faithful to take a different spiritual tack from the one they are enamored and used to. This will result in catching many of the faithful off-balance and many jaws to drop.

Mainstreaming stewardship will involve the rechanneling of

human and *financial resources* to a new program unbeknownst to many. The church builders will impel the Parish Pastoral Council (PPC), Lay Organizations, Movements, and Associations (LOMA), and Ministries to sign on to an alternative way of doing and being church. Accordingly, we should prepare for the inevitable that a small segment of the traditional leadership will rebel or, at the very least, push back.

By the time the parish priest and the Delta Force have established stewardship in the parish, they would have rattled the four walls of the house of worship and transmogrified community life beyond all recognition.

It is thus only prudent that before we start a revolution of this magnitude, we must know why we want to do this, what we intend to do, and how we can reinvent the parish in the image of stewardship.

To not do this is to play dice with ruin.

For that reason, the third step in the 7-grade hierarchical scale of building the stewardship church that loves the poor is for the Delta Force to **figure out the *Why, What & How* of Stewardship**.

In this step, the parish priest leads the Delta Force to come to grips with the Stewardship Program. They make clear in their minds the nuts and bolts of why to promote stewardship, what it is, and how to establish it in the parish.

The eventual result of this process is the manufacture of an *implementation plan*.

IMPLEMENTATION PLAN

The WHY of STEWARDSHIP

The *Why* of stewardship is the reason for the program's being, its purpose, the cause it is fighting for, its core ambition.

It is crucial to state this ambition in unambiguous, simple terms everybody can understand. If the Delta Force cannot make sense of why they are pushing stewardship, then the whole endeavor will fail and sink like a stone; if the faithful in the parish cannot latch on to why they should adopt stewardship, then no one would give two hoots about it.

The glittering, eye-popping fourfold increase in offertory giving, the rise of vast armies of volunteers, the creation of new outreach programs, and the strengthening of ministries are minutiae that come in the church's wake of becoming a stewardship church.

So why, indeed, stewardship?

As embers fly up from the flames, **we roll out the Stewardship Program** *to make disciples*.

There can be no wandering and straying from this canon, no hewing and hawing, nor can there be alternative opinions and positions. *Everyone in the Team must realize that building a stewardship church is about making disciples.*

Period.

This point must be clear as day to the Team and they must commit to this without reservation. The pastor must work like a dog to ensure everyone gets it. He must endeavor to help the team members who live in the shadow of this idea without grasping it see the effulgent light.

Only then can the Delta Team crack on.

Who is a Disciple?

If the *Why* of the Stewardship Program is to make disciples, then the church builders must take the meaning of *What makes a disciple a disciple*. Absent an operational definition and key performance indicators of success, the Stewardship Program risks never finding out if it accomplished what it should accomplish.

In the scientific community, an operational definition is a model or representation of an idea with enough specificities on processes so that others can replicate your research. For example, an operational definition of "anger" can be specific changes in heart rate, blood pressure, dilation of the pupils. If you define "anger" as an unpleasant burst of emotion we feel when mistreated, you are correct. But you are so ambiguous in your meaning that it will not be of value to empirical research.

The point is, **minus operational definitions of key terms, determining cause and effect relationships is *impossible*.** Does regular attendance in Sunday worship cause one to become a good disciple? We cannot answer this unless we have an operational definition of what a good disciple means.

I suspect that one of the underlying reasons the church crumples at making disciples is because she does not have an accepted, simple, and practical operational definition. If we don't know the signature characteristics or defining marks of a disciple, how can we make any mother's son one?

Let's say we designate "change in heart" as the mark of a disciple. But note that this inner phenomenon is not as amenable to the eye test as, say, the behavior of "praying." To thus designate "change in heart" as the main attestation of a disciple is to complicate the evaluation process. To designate "praying," on the other hand, as one of the marks of a disciple makes it easy for us to determine if the stewardship program is succeeding in making disciples or not.

For an operational definition of a disciple, therefore, it makes sense to designate *behavioral signifiers*—like praying, serving, and giving—as opposed to nonbehavioral signifiers, like empathy, honesty, and integrity.

Of course, we can also use these nonbehavioral factors but, since they can only be validated using inferential means, they complexify the appraisement process. It is therefore best and practicable to focus on *behaviors*.

Remember also to focus on only a few target behaviors. The surest way to sink the stewardship ship is to require aspiring disciples to change a hundred or more of their current behaviors.

Good luck with that!

The Traditional View

Before we craft an operational definition of discipleship, let us first look at the popular meaning of a disciple. In this tent, the ultraconservatives define a disciple as an adherent of the beliefs, rituals, and traditions of the Catholic Church. This is poles apart from our previous general characterization that a disciple is one who is committed to Jesus and his mission!

In the worst iteration of this paradigm, it reduced discipleship to religiosity. To its adherents, making disciples means making people religious; hence, the single-minded obsession with body counts at Sunday Mass, the Block Rosary, Procession of Saints, and whatnot.

In this universe, they deem religious practice as the apex conduct and ultimate manifestation of Christian maturity and perfection; thereupon, the alarming lack of concern or even curiosity to find out if the sacraments, prayers, and beliefs led to conversion and a new way of life that cares for others and the natural world.

All of this is in contraposition to the exhortations of *Lumen Gentium*, the Dogmatic Constitution of the Church, which says that the role of the laity is to make this world better: "The laity, by their very vocation, seek the kingdom of God by engaging in temporal affairs and by ordering them according to the plan of God" (no. 31).

An unintended cancerous outgrowth of this radical stress on religiosity is that schizophrenic Catholics who are thieves, liars, adulterers, and scoundrels from Monday to Saturday but saints on Sunday can convince themselves and others that they are, in fact, good disciples.

And what about the throng of pseudo-Christians who are unrepentant of their sins and failings, who are unreformed in their iniquitous ways but avail of the Sacrament of Reconciliation to wash away their moral failings? By virtue of their religiosity, they can say without batting an eyelash that they are, in fact, good disciples too.

There are undoubtedly more strenuous hurdles to clear for

those who aspire to become disciples than a regular observance of religious rituals! Religiosity is but a door that leads to a life renewed—a means to an end. Thus, religiosity can never be a howling success in and of itself.

Does that mean that stewardship depreciates the sacraments and prayers?

Indubitably not.

Make no mistake that stewardship embraces and promotes religiosity. But here is its idiosyncrasy—on top of religiosity, stewardship moves us to adopt a new spirituality that fosters a new way of life.

In stewardship, a disciple *not only embraces religiosity* **according to the traditional definition** *but also adopts a new spirituality* **that brings about a lifestyle that is life-giving.**

This is the stewardship exemplification.

The imperilment is that we are out of balance and in a dither with the terms *spirituality* and *way of life*. Still, let us put on hold our pursuit of an operational definition of discipleship and turn a few corners first to make things clearer.

I promise to circle back later to dispose of this hanging matter.

Unraveling Spirituality

There is a dark fog descending heavily in the air. I suspect this fearsome apparition has to do with the perplexing and abstract notions of *spirituality* and *way of life*. In that event, please allow me to try my best to unpack and air these two concepts, starting with spirituality.

But first, a warning.

The notion of *spirituality* is hard to pin down. It is like the carefree wind that eludes both deadfall traps and entanglement nets. No wonder we are unsatisfied when we attempt to define it with resolution and finality. Let me, instead, attempt to characterize it in broad strokes that will admit further additions and enlargements by others who are far wiser.

So here is a rough go of it: **Spirituality is the thirst for purpose**.

This ever-abiding thirstiness for meaning moves us from the well-aired morning to the star-filled night. It lingers in our hearts where it remains potent through the turning of the years, through the marching and passing of ages. It is a stubborn itch that stimulates our sum and substance, compelling us to seek without respite until the conundrum is satisfied.

The quest for purpose coerces us to go on a hunt that takes an eternity carrying us over land and tide, across ravines, over mountains dark. It thrusts us to relentlessly pursue and seize that which is not given freely, or that which does not come to all. We are driven by the prescience that it is only when this purpose is grasped and lived can we become who we are and who we are meant to be.

There can be no peace, no satisfaction in life with this whispered duty overlooked, this thirst unquenched. To not find our purpose, in plain English, is to be voodooed and bedeviled.

It is to live the life of the damned.

Who am I?

Why am I here?

What is my unique purpose in life?

These are the questions that plague all men of all lands, that haunt all women of all lands, that badger all children of all lands. These interrogations are about you and me but are beyond you and me. They hound us all and exempt no one, except those who inhabit the lowest existential planes where thought and reflection are barred and banned.

To find our purpose, we must knock down strapping walls of finitude that imprison us and keep us small. We must push back and stretch the thin but robust margins that separate and demarcate "me" from "others." We must climb to the highest peaks where clouds are born, to this place so high that the view *includes all of creation*—where the borders of "me" from the "not me" blur and disperse from perception.

In that immortal, fathomless, and inclusive perspective lie the answers to the enduring questions. **In that hallowed place dwells the unvarnished truth: Our lives are not our own. We are here not only for ourselves but also for others. We are more when we are together than alone. We are here to serve.**

With that sageness comes the dire gut feeling that we are only here on this earth for but a twinkling of an eye to manifest our purpose. Our inescapable mortality makes finding and manifesting our purpose a race against the clock.

Stewardship is, thus, attractive and a godsend to many seekers.

It takes them without a digression to this hard-to-reach dwelling where our ground of being is fused to the primal matrix of the universe. By pointing the answers to the big existential questions, stewardship helps the seekers find their footing in the cosmos.

It helps them find their marks.

To the identity question, *Who am I?* stewardship declares: **You are God's steward.**

Know in your bones that this is who we are. Everything we have —our material possessions, achievements, families, and lives—is from God. We are not owners of anything, but we are caretakers of everything. We are watchkeepers and custodians of all of God's abundant blessings.

To the mission question, *Why am I here?* stewardship intones: **You are here to care for all creation.**

Know in your heart that this is our overall purpose. We are all gifted and blessed to serve. We are called to nourish and grow our abundant blessings so we can release our gifts, creativity, and resources to care for all of humanity, the material world, and all of God's creatures in it.

To the specific mission question, *What is my unique purpose in life?* stewardship cannot give you a one-size-fits-all answer. That is because our specific mission in life depends on our unique capacities and contexts. Your unique purpose must be a bespoke suit that fits you and you alone. You have to figure this one out by yourself.

There is, however, a ballpark answer to that: **You are here to serve.**

How you serve, whom you serve, which abilities and blessings you summon from yourself to uplift others and the world all depend on your inimitable circumstances and station in life.

If you are a teacher, your specific mission might be to instill the longing for lifelong learning in your students. If you are a jeepney driver, it might be to transport your passengers safely. If you are a manufacturer, your mission might be to provide products that make life better for your customers. If you are the eldest in the brood, it might be to ensure all your younger siblings finish school. If you are a parent who is as poor as a church mouse, your life mission might be to provide food for your children.

Again, the specific mission varies according to your abilities, resources, and circumstances. But it always comes down to service or the generous sharing of our talents and blessings to make this a better world.

When we say and do all, our lives are inquiries with one resolution—love, service, taking care of each other and the world.

And then, we die.

The Stewardship Way of Life

Now onward to the unpacking of the other notion that confounds and mocks us: What is the stewardship way of life?

In stewardship, this proffered way of life is characterized as one filled with prayer, service, and giving. This is the bearing and mannerism God asks us to assume 24/7. This is how we are to live on a moment-to-moment, day-to-day basis.

Notice, stewardship strives for changing lifestyles—new habits and recurring patterns of behaviors—and does not put too much weight on the *occasional* good thought, kind word, or good deed, no matter how grand. Sporadic acts of kindness are well and fine, but because they come few and far between, they are not our real, incarnated dwellings. They are perhaps happy, accidental excursions from our regular tarnished states of being.

To assign momentousness to individual instances of good behaviors, therefore, is to lose sight of the forest for the trees. It opens the door a crack for rancorous fugitives to enter and take over our moral judgment and bearing.

Turnover in your mind what happens when we are indecisive with an inveterate liar. On the rare occasions that the man speaks the truth, do we entertain the alternative notion that he is perhaps a truth-teller? What about the unreserved misogynist? Do we whip out a substitute appraisal of his character when he is kind to his mother, wife, or sister? And the dead clock that tells the right time twice a day, do we declare that gadget good enough to set the times of our lives by?

One swallow does not make a summer, and the occasional good deed does not make a noble character.

Let us sink the trifles of erratic good deeds and stand on the solid ground of lifestyle or way of life. Let us not rise in homage to the occasional display of kindheartedness, no matter how admirable, but celebrate long-lasting good habits, recurring patterns of good thoughts, words, and deeds instead, no matter how simple.

After all, it is not what we do *now and then* that defines us. **It is what we do *all the time* that makes us who we are.**

Therefore as stewards and disciples, we should make prayer, service, and giving a full-time concern and a lifelong undertaking. We should make this lifestyle our dominant approach to life under the Lord's expansive blue sky.

That is how we flourish—like wild grasses on the fields.

Operational Definition of a Disciple

Without more ado, allow me to return to the interrupted business of devising an operational definition of discipleship for the Stewardship Program.

52

The Definition of a Disciple:

> 1. A disciple is one whose way of life is marked by the habits of prayer, service, and giving. (*Behavior*)
>
> 2. And this way of life is rooted in the stewardship identity and mission to care for all of creation. (*Purpose and mission*)

Note that our operational definition comprises two intertwined parts. The initial portion makes use of behaviors and is thus accessible to direct observation and measurement. The second part is about purpose and mission, or new ways of being. It is incorporeal and must therefore be fathomed using indirect means, such as interviews, testimonies, or questionnaires.

The second point is crucial because many people pray, serve, and give. But in as far as their actions are driven not by stewardship but by selfish motivations, it means they are still a few colors short of a rainbow. As St. Paul said, "If I give away all I have, and if I deliver my body to be burned, but have not love, I gain nothing" (1 Corinthians 13:3).

We are on the straight and narrow path to Christian impeccability only when our way of life is marked with prayer, service, and giving; and, this way of life is rooted in stewardship identity and mission to care for all creation.

Indeed, actions and behavioral indicators are important, but spirituality or what moves us (although invisible to the eyes) is equally important. In stewardship, **the whole nine yards is a lifestyle filled with *recurring behaviors* of prayer, service, and giving; and, spirituality *rooted* in stewardship identity and mission**.

In a word, it is about *a new way of life* and *a new way of being*.

But how in the world does the Stewardship Program help the faithful develop the habits of prayer, service, and giving? How does it promote the adoption of the stewardship identity and mission?

You must be side-bent, head-curious by now about the *What*

of the Stewardship Program. Tuck your trousers' end inside your ratty high-cut Converse sneakers and let's get to it!

The WHAT of STEWARDSHIP

The *What* of stewardship is a basic description of the program. This includes the Stewardship Program's (a) target goals, (b) programs offered, (c) key performance indicators, and (d) mechanisms that it employs to get things done.

Goals

Let us begin this section by identifying the desired goals or outcomes. *It is only when we know what we want to achieve that we can determine how best to accomplish it.* Minus that clarity of means and ends, we could end up with feeble plans that espouse absurd actions, such as climbing trees to catch fish.

To dispel recklessness and confusion later on, we must now ask ourselves what we hope to accomplish with this Stewardship Program.

To the pioneers, the most often articulated Stewardship Program Goals are

> 1. **Personal Conversion:** To make disciples. (And the best practice is to operationally define a disciple as one whose way of life is brimming with prayer, service, and giving; and, this way of life is rooted in stewardship identity and mission.)
>
> 2. **Institutional Renewal:** To build a praying, serving, and giving church that makes disciples.

After you spell out what the program is striving for, the next step is to determine how best to realize these outcomes. What do we do to snag the stated goals?

This is where the individual Stewardship Programs of Time, Talent, and Treasure come in.

Programs

The Stewardship of Time or Prayer

"Pray constantly, give thanks in all circumstances; for this is the will of God in Christ Jesus for you." (1 Thessalonians 5:17-18)

The Stewardship of Time (or Stewardship of Prayer) Program is the starting point in the journey to make disciples and renew the church. It is also the firm foundation on which we build the Stewardship Programs of Talent and Treasure.

Time is a valuable gift from God.

To our detriment, however, we think that our time is as inexhaustible as the ocean. We waste it willy-nilly on foolish pursuits and childish things. We delude ourselves that time will never run out. We keep our fingers crossed, hoping there is enough sand left in the hourglass to rectify and amend our ways.

Sadly, the truth is we are embers drifting in the night, here only for the briefest of moments. We could be hale and hearty now but gone in a flash tomorrow. Only a fool thinks that time will never run out.

In the Stewardship of Time program, we reflect on how we use this God-given gift of time. Are we squandering it away? Or are we using it wisely?

We are gracefully nudged to set aside a portion of our time to give back to God in prayer so we may get to know him, love him, know his will and take part in the inbreaking of his reign. It asks us to do all that out of gratitude and love.

The twin goals of the Stewardship of Time program are to help us adopt

- The habit of prayer so we can deepen our relationship with God
- The stewardship identity and mission

The Stewardship of Talent or Service

"As each has received a gift, employ it for one another,

as good stewards of God's varied grace." (1 Peter 4:10)

In the Stewardship of Talent (or Stewardship of Service) Program, it asks us to confront the threefold task of

- Discovering our God-given talents
- Nurturing and developing our talents
- Sharing our talents—out of love and justice—with others, especially the poor and downtrodden

The targeted outcomes of this program are to help us adopt

- The habit of service or the regular practice of lending a hand to uplift others, our family, community, and church while expecting nothing in return
- The stewardship identity and mission

The Stewardship of Treasure

> "Do not lay up for yourselves treasures on earth,
> where moth and rust consume
> and where thieves break in and steal, but lay up
> for yourselves treasures in heaven,
> where neither moth nor rust consumes and
> where thieves do not break in and steal.
> For where your treasure is, there will your
> heart be also." (Matthew 6:19-21)

Contrary to popular belief, the Stewardship of Treasure is not only about the tithe or giving 10 percent of your income back to God; *it is about our relationship with all our material blessings and how we use them.*

Where we put our treasures reveals what we think is important and the state of our hearts. Do you spend a lot on jewelry and fast cars? Do you allot a portion of your income to charity? Do you help a relative pay for her education?

This program helps us develop

- The habit of sharing our material blessings to take care of others and restore the world

- The stewardship identity and mission

By What Measure?

How can we tell if the Stewardship Programs of Time, Talent, and Treasure are succeeding or not? How do we know if they are re-invigorating the institutional church or not?

That is what key performance indicators are for.

Before we do the whole kit and caboodle, let us step aside a moment and note that the **Catholic Bishops' Conference of the Philippines** is pushing for the removal of the *Arancel System* in the Philippines.

The *Arancel System* refers to the archaic practice of collecting fixed fees for the sacraments of baptism, matrimony, confirmation, and other services (e.g., the offering of Mass intentions). It is a residue of the 333 years of Spanish colonial rule in the Philippines.

The Second Plenary Council of the Philippines (PCP II) in 1991, stated: "Tithing, after a good pastoral catechesis, shall be introduced with the end in view of the gradual abolition of the Arancel System" (no. 118).

It has been 30 years since PCP II, yet the campaign to do away with the *Arancel* is still ongoing. This oldfangled custom is obviously discriminatory against the poor who do not have the means to pay the fees. We must not rest until we make the sacraments freely available to one and all. That is why dismantling the *Arancel System* should be one of the Stewardship Programs' key ambitions.

To return to the topic of success indicators, we need markers that can be observed, measured, and improved. Without these concrete guideposts, the church builders cannot manage the iterative evaluation process that leads to organizational adjustments and refinements.

What I will present are the Key Result Areas (KRAs) used by the pioneer builders of stewardship churches to estimate their programs' success. It is from these that the Delta Force can identify the *qualitative* and *quantitative* success indicators.

Key Result Areas

1. The Delta Force is leading the charge to promote the spirituality of stewardship and its programs.

2. Replaced the *Arancel System* with voluntary giving.

3. More parishioners are praying, serving, and giving.

Possible success indicators: 5% increase in attendance in Sunday Masses; 20% increase in offertory giving; 25% increase in the membership of Ministries and LOMA.

4. The PPC, LOMA, Ministries, and the BECs have adopted the Stewardship Program.

Possible success indicators: 80% of PPC, LOMA, and Ministries —both leaders and members—have undergone stewardship formation and are pledging.

5. Formation and Pledging are implemented all year round.

6. The poor have free access to the sacraments and other church services.

7. Systems that promote transparency and accountability are in place.

How do we determine if the program is fit as a fiddle or dead as a doornail?

We examine the success indicators housed under the roofs of the KRAs and see how they stack up against actual performance. If program performance measures up, then our program is up to snuff; if it falls flat against the indicators, then we have to investigate the reasons behind the foul-ups. We can, thereafter, use these newfound revelations to tweak and revamp the program and make it better.

To reckon if the program is proceeding according to plan, pin your hopes on the devices of monitoring and evaluation. This is the blue-ribbon way to make programs better—not by guesswork, not by the reading of tea leaves, not by the inspection of the entrails of sacrificed animals.

Hammer and Anvil

I would like to say that the Stewardship Program employs two instruments that work side by side to make disciples and revivify the church.

1. **Formation or Education Process.** Through this apparatus, aspirants are taught the incorporeal of stewardship —identity, purpose, meaning, mission, and vision.

2. **Pledge or Covenant.** This device helps the faithful develop a way of life awash with prayer, service, and giving.

The best practice of the stewardship pioneers is to use both mechanisms of formation and pledges *simultaneously, extensively, and continually.*

In contrast, those who came to naught deployed Formation only at the start of their campaign to promote stewardship in the parish. They unceremoniously abandoned it afterward when the pledged funds rolled in.

The quintessential outcome of this one-handed approach is that, even though some parishes raked in a considerable amount of ready money at the outset, their Stewardship Programs eventually ran aground and petered out.

Why that happened is not obscure. By overlooking formation and focusing only on Treasure, the off-beam church builders corroborated the parishioners' worst suspicions that they were only using stewardship to make money and not disciples. No surprise that this led to the rapid loss of popular support for stewardship.

Thus, the program's eventual decline to inconsequentiality!

The HOW of STEWARDSHIP

Stepladder Technique

As the last point of this chapter, we come to the practical concern of *How* to put up the Stewardship Program in the church. Naturally, you cannot get to where you want to go without deciphering how you are going to get there.

To triumphantly roll out the Stewardship Program in your parish, think of ripples in the water. When you throw a pebble in a pond, it dislodges water only at the drop point; nonetheless, the initial disturbance subsequently propagates outwards to disturb a larger and larger area until it occupies the entire pond.

That is the best practice on how to roll out the Stewardship Programs: Start small before you swing a bat at big. Embark on the simple before you lock horns with the complicated. Kickoff on a small section of the church before you have a go at the entire parish.

I call this one-rung-at-a-time process the *Stepladder Technique* and show below how the pioneers carried it out in their parishes.

The Stewardship Program's Stepladder Technique

    A. Rolling out the Stewardship Program

        1. Implement Stewardship of Time or Prayer first.

        2. Follow with Stewardship of Talent or Service.

        3. Finally, carry out Stewardship of Treasure.

    B. Expanding your Target Groups

        1. Start with the key parish leaders: PPC members and heads of LOMA and the different Ministries.

        2. Then move forward and buckle down on all the members of the above groups.

        3. After that, tackle the regular parishioners and Sunday Mass-goers.

        4. Lastly, focus on the margins to cover the Basic Ecclesial Communities (BECs) and chapels.

PARTING REFRAIN

The Delta Force must sail through the *Why, What & How* process if it is to make inroads in rolling out the Stewardship Programs in their parishes. They must invest time and energy to get the details right and not skedaddle through this step just to tick the box.

By figuring out the basics in your implementation plan before jumping into the fray, the core leaders get their mitts on what they need to succeed. This is a gainful step that invigorates the Teams' chances of successfully building a stewardship church that loves the poor.

I close this chapter with this triplet that came to me in the middle of a sweltering, tropical night:

Victory at no time comes to the unprepared.

Victory often comes to those who prepare.

Victory unfailingly comes to those who overprepare.

TAKEAWAYS

The third step in building a stewardship church that loves the poor is to **make an implementation plan that comes to grips with the *Why, What & How* of the program**.

Why Put Up the Stewardship Program?

To make disciples and renew the church.

What Is the Operational Definition of a Disciple?

A disciple is one whose way of life is marked by prayer, service, and giving; and, this way of life is rooted in stewardship identity and mission.

What Are the Stewardship Program's Target Outcomes?

1. Personal Conversion: To make disciples.

2. Institutional Renewal of the Church: To make a praying, serving, and giving church that makes disciples.

What Are the Program's Success Indicators?

1. The Delta Force is leading the charge to promote the

spirituality of stewardship and its programs.

2. Replaced the *Arancel System* with voluntary giving.

3. More parishioners are praying, serving, and giving.

4. The PPC, LOMA, Ministries, and the BECs have adopted the Stewardship Programs.

5. Formation and Pledging are implemented all year round.

6. The poor have free access to the sacraments and other services of the church.

7. Systems that promote transparency and accountability are in place.

What Are the Program's Key Components?

- Stewardship of Time
- Stewardship of Talent
- Stewardship of Treasure

What Are the Apparatuses Used to Make the Various Stewardship Programs Effective?

- Formation or education
- System of Pledges

How to Roll Out the Stewardship Program?

- Key implementer - Delta Force
- Stepladder technique in implementing the Time, Talent, and Treasure programs
- Stepladder technique in taking in the various target groups

STEP 4: LAUNCH A MASSIVE EDUCATION CAMPAIGN

THE FOURTH STEP IN BUILDING a stewardship church that loves the poor is to **launch a massive Stewardship Education Campaign** that will saturate and immerse the whole of the parish from head to heel.

The natural urge is to dive in headfirst and figure it out along the way. But the prudent way is we make an implementation plan first before we discharge the Education Campaign.

Why are you launching this Campaign and for what purpose? What needs to be implemented? How is it to be rolled out? Who handles what? These are the key things the Delta Force must sort out and pick in their brains before they cross the Rubicon.

Before we get into that, we need to take a brief detour on pedagogy—the practice and method of teaching.

A TALE OF TWO APPROACHES

A word to the wise, this subject is as vast and as deep as the ocean and, if we are not careful, we might end up lost at sea. For that reason, we will delimit ourselves to one pedagogical concern that I think we need to grasp to become effective instructors of stewardship—our attitudes toward teaching.

I hold helping others, especially those in most need, overcome ignorance and spiritual denseness to be the highest task. I take my hat off and give high props to teachers, mentors, and coaches who help people develop their unrealized talents, teaching them to find their voices and sing their songs. I believe **these teachers are at the coalface in the dog-eat-dog struggle to overcome the distempers and infirmities of the dark hour so we may realize a better, kinder world.**

I view all who volunteer their time and talent to the Stewardship Education Campaigns from this extolling attitude. There are, however, teachers who are downright inept.

The focus question is: *What differentiates successful teachers from those who come to grief?*

There are the usual explanations, say, competency in communication, interpersonal skills, the abilities to design and manage courses, and so forth. These factors matter. What blows our minds, though, is how attitudes toward teaching are game changers.

It is a revelation to see that the teachers' attitudes and views about the teaching process, their role, and their expectations of the learners shape how they design and conduct the teaching sessions. No one from the pioneer stewardship builders summoned the pedagogical terms *learner-centered* and *teacher-centered* approaches, but the unlettered proponents of the two factions were engaged in a pitched battle to determine which approach could win the most hearts and minds.

Teacher-Centered Approach

The adherents of the teacher-centered approach see themselves as authority figures who possess the knowledge and chops they wish to transfer to their fledgling students. **They regard their students as empty and passive receptacles of learning.** Ergo, the teachers' radical dependence on the most direct way of transferring knowledge via lectures to the exclusion of other teaching devices.

Memorization and prowess on the surface nature of knowledge is a big part of teacher-centered education. It is, unfortunately, not as cherished by the students, nor is it as effective. The array of learners preferred the opportunity to play an active role in meaning-making. They favored the license to share their experiences with others, and they longed for the pleasure of learning from their peers.

Learner-Centered Approach

The disciples of the learner-centered approach see themselves as facilitators of learning. **They regard their students as active learners who make up their minds, ask questions, express opinions, and share their experiences.** They likewise use lectures. But in addition to that, they employ various teaching tools that facilitate reflection and peer-to-peer engagement, such as open forums, small group discussions, and practical assignments.

When all is said and done, the learner-centered approach is the clear winner in this war of teaching methodologies.

The pioneer builders who espoused this learner-centered approach to teaching stewardship got it done with minor hitch and begot higher satisfaction ratings from their students. This resounding endorsement led to higher attendance and participation in parish-sponsored activities, plus more observable behavioral changes in the learners.

THE ROLE OF CULTURE IN LEARNING

Another worthwhile thing to bring up here is culture. Culture plays a significant role in learning. Those who use the native language and explain abstract stewardship concepts using local cultural examples and values often make the grade, with no trouble, while those who do not, struggle.

A case in point is *Pananabangan (communio,* which means God's union and fellowship with his people), the formation program of the Archdiocese of Lingayen, Dagupan. It adopts and integrates aspects of the local culture in its instructions on how to live the life of a good steward.

In a nutshell, these are the **two foundational things you must**

keep in hand to succeed as a stewardship instructor:

> 1. Adopt the learner-centered approach to teaching that employs interactive teaching tools. This encourages peer-to-peer engagement that fosters learning.

> 2. Use the local culture to expedite learning.

Don't worry if a lot of this is above your head for now. We will bring these abstract concepts together to practical comportment when we design a stewardship workshop towards the end of this chapter.

THE FOUR BATTLEGROUNDS

This chapter is about

✓ **Creating new mechanisms**

✓ **Changing congregational habits**

The two other undertakings are

- Setting new church priorities
- Promoting a new culture that cements the changes

IMPLEMENTATION PLAN

Now, forward to the key task of devising the implementation plan for the massive Stewardship Education Campaign.

The WHY of STEWARDSHIP CAMPAIGN

Let's start with *Why* we are launching the education campaign in the first place, why it is important, and how things bend over rearwards to fit in the overall goal of making disciples.

This massive education campaign is to make sure that all church leaders and the large part of parish worshippers get a comprehensible hang of stewardship. The challenge is to make the stewardship concept clear so that nothing about it is left in the air to impede its popular adoption.

The WHAT of STEWARDSHIP CAMPAIGN

The education campaign is a fundamental mechanism to realize this big-league goal of making disciples. Here are the Success Indicators often adopted by the pioneer builders apropos the Stewardship Education Campaign.

Success Indicators

1. All leaders and members of the Parish Pastoral Council (PPC), Lay Organizations, Movements, and Associations (LOMA), and Ministries have taken the stewardship workshops.

2. All Basic Ecclesial Communities (BECs) and chapel leaders have taken the stewardship workshops.

3. The parishioners are aware of stewardship.

From the metrics above, the Delta Force could now appraise themselves if they did a bang-up job or not.

The Stewardship Workshop

The Stewardship Campaign requires a spate of teaching devices from workshops, seminars, testimonials, Sunday homilies, and informal talks to stewardship articles on the parish newsletter and bulletin boards and posts of stewardship happenings on social media.

I will, however, focus on the chief instrument in the education campaign: The Stewardship Workshop. **This Workshop is the preeminent teaching maneuver to help parishioners gain foundational knowledge of stewardship**. It is a series of organized and planned formation events whereby an intensive teaching experience of lectures, group reflections, and discussions is given to a small group of 10 to 25 people to improve their stewardship understanding and practice.

Many upcoming stewardship implementers think that the

Stewardship Workshop is all about the PowerPoint presentation and an excellent public speaker. They presume that if they could only get their hands on a proper self-contained instruction on stewardship and the right speaker, then everything will roll out to the sound of beating drums and a shower of flowers.

While excellent public speakers and proper stewardship modules are vital, in reality, they are just two of many necessary factors that must come together for the workshop experience to make the cut. You may have the best speaker with a marvelous stewardship PowerPoint presentation, but if there is no opportunity in the workshop for participants to reflect, interact with their peers, and take part in meaning-making, then the participants might still miss the mark.

So you won't get lost in unnecessary pedagogical entanglements, here is a list of the best practices in conducting stewardship workshops. I also supplied a sample Stewardship Workshop Program to illustrate how these best practices are cobbled together into an integrated process that facilitates engagement and learning.

Conducting the Stewardship Workshop

1. Use the parish and community's local culture

- Use the local language and culture.
- Compare and contrast stewardship values to existing local cultural values.

2. Make abstract ideas concrete

- Explain by using examples taken from the local way of life.
- Ask ordinary people to share their stewardship experience and journey.

3. Provide or use learning materials

- Handouts
- PowerPoint presentations
- Videos

4. Use processes that encourage engagements

- Small group discussions
- Open forums
- Social interactions
- Personal testimonies
- Assignments or tasks to accomplish later

Stewardship Workshop Program

If designing a stewardship workshop seems as complicated as the play of light and shade, don't worry. Here is the promised stripped-down program to create a sweet process conducive to learning:

A. Preliminaries

1. Opening prayer

2. Welcome and Backgrounder by the Pastor

- Why are we here?
- Why were you invited?
- Why stewardship, and why does the parish want to become a stewardship church?

3. Self-Introductions by Everyone

- State your name.
- Say something about yourself.
- Why are you here?
- What are your expectations for the workshop?

4. Expectation Check and Flow of the Day by the Facilitator

- Note which of the group's expectations can be met.
- Note which expectations are beyond this workshop.
- Give the flow of the day or workshop program so the participants know what to expect.
- Introduce the speaker.

B. Main Input by the Speaker

What is stewardship? What advantages and benefits does stewardship bring to people, churches, and communities? What hinders us from adopting it? Practical tips on how to become a better steward.

C. Testimonial

Ask someone to share her or his stewardship experience.

1. Have her introduce and say something about herself.

2. How was she introduced to stewardship?

3. What was her life like before stewardship? And after becoming a steward?

D. Open Forum

Focus Questions: What was clear in the stewardship talk? What needs more clarification?

E. Small-Group Discussion

1. Focus Questions: What struck me in the stewardship talk? What challenged me? New insights? What is the one thing I can do to become a better steward?

2. Reporting: Ask one or two people to report their small group discussion to the main body.

3. Synthesis: Summarize the talk's key points and the important matters raised in the small group sharing.

F. Assignments

1. Share some things you learned here with a family member or a neighbor.

2. Post pictures or some of your comments about this workshop on your social media.

G. Closing Ceremony

1. Closing remarks from the Parish priest

2. Closing prayer and blessing

Online Encounters

The Stewardship Workshop is effective because it promotes learning in a social environment. Unfortunately, the pandemic has obviated face-to-face encounters and prodded the wholesale shift to remote learning.

Whereas remote learning is a powerful medium, it brings many challenges nonetheless. Access to the internet, bandwidth issues, proper equipment, and technical know-how are just a few of the myriad stumbling blocks that are immanent to online conferences.

It is still possible to engage the participants in a workshop format using this new medium. The trick is to break the body into small groups so they can engage the focus questions or discussion prompts in a more intensive and participative manner. Most platforms for remote meetings have this utility called *breakout rooms* for this purpose. I highly recommend that you use this feature to stimulate deeper peer-to-peer engagements and collaborations.

Who Will Run the Stewardship Workshops?

Most pioneer builders choose to delegate the responsibility of running the workshops to the Parish Formation Team if there is one extant in their parishes. This is a reasonable course of action since seminars and workshops are right up the alley of the Parish Formation Team. The handover of responsibility is also not as hard as it seems because, the odds are, some members of the Parish Formation Team are also members of the Delta Force.

Others choose to start from scratch. They sidestep the Parish Formation Team and assign members of the Delta Force to create a freshly baked Stewardship Formation Team to oversee the education campaign. This maneuver often leads to strains and collisions between the new-sprung Stewardship Formation Team and the long-established Parish Formation Team.

Because no one wants to foul one's own nest, I assume those

who take this route do so for compelling reasons.

Regardless of how you go about it, this Formation Team must collaborate with the Delta Force and the pastor to ensure that everyone is on the same page.

Here is an enumeration of the **Roles and Tasks in the Stewardship Workshop**:

Facilitators

- Introduce the speaker, parish priest, etc. in the workshop
- Introduce what comes next and summarize what has gone before
- Run the Open Forum and Sharing Sessions
- Ensure that the workshop starts and ends on time
- Ensure that the people are paying attention during the workshop
- Ensure that everyone speaks

Speakers

- Give the main stewardship talk
- Answer questions and make clarifications

Workshop Organizers

- Take care of the invitations and follow-ups
- Secure the workshop venues
- Provide technical support and provide the workshop supplies
- Provide snacks

Secretary

- Makes the workshop registration forms
- Encodes the personal data of all workshop attendees
- Notes down questions and remarks raised in the workshops
- Takes the minutes of all Formation Team meetings
- Sends the meeting minutes to all Formation Team members

Finance Officer

- Secures finances needed for the workshops
- Ensures all financial transactions are properly documented
- Collects all receipts
- Gives regular reports

Life witness sharers

Share their stewardship journey

Parish priest

- Welcomes the participants and gives an overview of the significance of stewardship to the parish
- Answers questions
- Gives the closing remarks and final blessing

The Pastor's Key Role

If there is one pure and incorruptible determinant of success that we can count on, it is the parish priest's participation. If the pastor is present, the participants will most likely rate the workshop experience a slam dunk. If he is not there, the participants might think this is just a flavor-of-the-month undertaking that comes and goes with the passing of the seasons.

The workshops may take an immoderate amount of the pastor's time, but his presence there is crucial—*it signals to the parishioners that he is at the helm of this massive turnabout in the parish's life.* He must endeavor to always be present in the workshops and use these occasions to forge lasting bonds of significance with his church leaders and community.

The HOW of STEWARDSHIP CAMPAIGN

This truth is as old as the hills: Start small before you go big; walk before you run.

Try out the venture on a small corner of the parish to minimize the repercussions of mistakes and shortcomings while gaining invaluable experience in execution. Gather what went well and why, as well as what did not go well and why. It is only after you have figured out the reasons behind the slipups and rectified them that you pump up the volume and go parish-wide.

What does this mean in practical terms?

It means aiming to bring around an ever-spreading target group of possible stewardship converts from the leaders in the parish to the parishioners in the periphery. **Think of it as casting a series of ever-widening nets to snap bigger and bigger catches,** *stopping only when you have captured the entire parish.*

Take the plunge by offering the Stewardship Workshop to the parish leaders first. Start with the members of the Parish Pastoral Council (PPC), the leaders of Lay Organizations, Movements, and Associations (LOMA), and the heads of the Ministries. Follow that up by conducting workshops for the members.

Having secured the leaders in the center, you now turn your gaze to the margins and cast your wider net there. Offer the workshops to the chapel leaders and small Christian communities or BECs.

Now that all the parish leaders in the center and the periphery have undergone the Stewardship Workshops, you can now offer them to the public. Open wide the doors and welcome all who wish to learn about stewardship.

At this juncture, you have made the basic stewardship workshop the common experience that informs and unites all leaders and parishioners in your church.

Congratulations, you have swept the entire parish along the moving and refreshing waters of stewardship renewal!

TAKEAWAYS

The fourth step in building a stewardship church that loves the poor is to **launch a massive Stewardship Education Campaign.**

Why Launch a Stewardship Formation Campaign?

To help the faithful in the parish understand the brass tacks of stewardship.

What Is This Stewardship Education Campaign?

It is a series of formation events, like talks, homilies, social media posts, and information dissemination designed to teach stewardship throughout the parish. Its main education campaign apparatus is the Stewardship Workshop.

What Are the Best Practices in Running the Workshops?

- Uses the local culture and language
- Uses processes and mechanisms that encourage engagement in learning and peer-to-peer interactions
- Lay witnessing
- The pastor's active participation

Who Will Run the Workshops?

Either you create a Stewardship Formation Team or you delegate the responsibility to the existing Parish Formation Team.

How Do You Roll It Out in the Parish?

Start by offering the basic Stewardship Workshops to all the leaders in both the parish center and periphery. Then make it available to all who wish to take it.

STEP 5: ROLL OUT THE PLEDGES

I AM A FLAWED PERSON. I have committed more than my fair share of sins, indiscretions, and imprudence to make a colossal muck of my life. Hard to admit, but I have—as often as not—tried to improve myself and failed. This pursuit of becoming our most elevated selves is severe, overwhelming, and prone to entanglements and failure.

When I take a good squint at it, I say that this project to better myself is an ill-fated undertaking akin to the summer nights I spent during my childhood counting the stars in the sky with my paternal grandfather. Somewhere along the way, I would lose count, so I would start again from one. Following this, I would lose tally at a later point; and I would do it over again, ad infinitum.

I, therefore, spent ages searching for wisdom so I could turn over the tainted pages of my life and start afresh. This is the simple aspiration that kept me hopeful through the turning of the seasons. Thank God I learned the secret of how to reconstruct myself and become a new person through the Stewardship Program.

It is thus with exuberant joy that I share this knowledge with you: **What you do *time after time* forms the person you are, the values you hold dear, the beliefs you swear by, and the unique consciousness you inhabit.**

The transcendental patchwork of mental, physical, spiritual, emotional, and moral identities, personas, and constitutions that make up our person is, in reality, the summation of our habits. The goulash of achievements and ruination we manifest in the world is but a stack up of the behavioral and thought patterns we repeat most often—what we think, do, and say is what we materialize and externalize.

It is our habits that determine who we are and our impact on the rest of humanity and the world. If you want to turn your life around and make this world a better place, revise your habits.

The formula for self-transformation is through the *accretion of small actions oft-repeated* time and again. It is counterintuitive, but radical transformations are often the byproducts of small steps and marginal evolutions. **This is because big change rarely sticks.** To make that plain, think of all the life-changing, world-altering New Year's resolutions you've made that died on the vine and bit the dust.

While some habits can be obstructive, such as wasting entire evenings binge-watching our favorite streaming series or *telenovelas* when you should work on your pastoral report or wash dishes, other habits can push you to higher levels of goodness and competency. Sticking to a healthy plant-based diet, for instance, will ensure that you will stay in good nick in your old age while you do the planet a good turn.

It is not rocket science. If you want to become a well-informed person, read at least ten pages of a good book each day. If you want to be in good trim, walk 30 minutes every day. If you want to turn into a good-hearted individual, treat others gracefully a few times a day.

I know it sounds dull and commonplace. We half expect that profound wisdom is revealed to the sound of celestial trumpets, but there it is, clear as a bell: *The shortcut to our elevated selves is by getting rid of bad habits and adopting good ones.*

This brings us to the next step in building a stewardship church that loves the poor: **Roll out the pledges!**

On the matter of changing the faithful's habits and behaviors, this apparatus is as good as gold.

THE FOUR BATTLEGROUNDS

This chapter is about

✓ **Changing the habits of the congregation**

The other three battlegrounds are

- Shifting the church's priorities
- Setting up institutional mechanisms
- Promoting a new culture that will shore up the changes

IMPLEMENTATION PLAN

The WHY of PLEDGING

WHY do we ask the congregation to pledge?

We do this to help churchgoers become disciples. Keep in mind that the basic behavioral hallmark of a disciple or a good steward is a way of life filled with prayer, service, and giving.

If you are like me who lacks the willpower and self-discipline to keep at it until I achieve my goals, then the convention of pledges is a godsend. Pledges beef us up by making it pricey to capitulate on our ambitions and goals. When we give our word of honor and memorialize it in writing, it is no longer just a matter of praying, serving, and giving out of whim or passing pious disposition. **It is now a covenant with God and the community.**

It is this unpalatable prospect of breaking our vows that induces us to hold the line. Because we need all the help we can get to stay on the straight and narrow, this additional encumbrance is, exactly, what most of us well-intentioned slackers need.

The WHAT of PLEDGING

Stewardship Pledges

The pioneer builders roll out three stewardship commitments: (1)

the commitment on Time or Prayer stipulates the time the pledger will devote to private and public prayer, (2) the oath on Talent is a listing of how the pledger vows to serve the church, and (3) the promise on Treasure is the amount of money the pledger will donate to the church.

Here are garden-variety examples of the commitment cards:

Stewardship of Prayer
Commitment Card
Name of the Parish or Church

Out of thankfulness to the Father, I promise
to pray for the Good News of total salvation
to be shared to everyone in our parish:

5 minutes a day	_____
10 minutes a day	_____
15 minutes a day	_____
20 minutes a day	_____
Other	_____

Name _____

Address _____

Email _____

Cellphone _____

Signature _____

"Rejoice always, pray without ceasing, give thanks
in all circumstances; for this is the will of God in
Christ Jesus for you." (1 Thessalonians 5:16-18)

Stewardship of Talent
Commitment Card
Name of the Parish Church

I offer my talent as a living sacrifice to God. I pledge to serve in:

Worship
___ Altar Server
___ Eucharistic Minister
___ Greeter
___ Other (specify): _____

Education
___ BEC
___ Catechist
___ Stewardship
___ Others (specify): _____

Temporalities
___ Bereavement
___ Ministry for the Sick
___ Social Action
___ Other (specify): _____

Service
___ Church Cleaning
___ Equipment
___ Finance Council
___ Others (specify): _____

Youth
___ Altar Server
___ Eucharistic Minister
___ Greeter
___ Other (specify): _____

Lay Organizations
___ BEC
___ Catechist
___ Stewardship
___ Others (specify): _____

Name _____
Address _____
Email _____
Cellphone _____

Signature _____

"Practice hospitality ungrudgingly to one another. As each has received a gift, employ it for one another, as good stewards of God's varied grace." (1 Peter 4:9-10)

Stewardship of Treasure
Commitment Card
Name of the Parish or Church

I thank God for all the blessings He has bestowed upon me and my family. As a good steward, I offer this financial commitment to support the mission to make disciples.

I pledge the amount of _____ a week.

Name   _____
Address   _____
Email   _____
Cellphone _____

Signature _____

"Do not neglect to do good and to share what you have, for such sacrifices are pleasing to God." (Hebrews 13:16)

Vital Elements in Administration

Below are some of our stewardship pioneers' best practices on administering pledges.

Put Up or Strengthen Institutional Mechanisms to Harness Talents and Money for Mission

Set up the mechanisms on how the church will release the potency of incoming volunteers and financial resources for the mission *before* you hand out the pledge forms.

Does the church have prayer and religious events lined up to accommodate those who will volunteer to pray more? Will the church give away free rosaries and prayer books to teach people how to pray? Are the Lay Organizations, Movements, and Associations (LOMA), Basic Ecclesial Communities (BECs), and Ministries ready to take in the influx of fresh volunteers? And what about the money and gifts—is there a plan on how to use these to make disciples?

The worst-case scenario is for the Delta Force to have oodles of volunteers and piles of fresh funds at their disposal yet remain clueless on how to press them in service of the mission.

Transparency and Accountability

It is vital to keep everyone in the loop regarding the *What's what of the Stewardship Program*. This is most especially true with treasure. Money is a natural fault line for conflicts and disagreements, so the Team must manage it masterfully.

The best practice is to live by the twin standards of transparency and accountability.

At the heart of transparency is the regular sharing of financial information with the congregation. This means posting quarterly reports on how much money was raised, where the money was spent, the donors' names, and the current financial status of the church. This practice not only affirms the givers but also builds trust that the church is on the level, and everything is by the book. (Some donors, however, wish to remain anonymous as they hold to the Filipino value that giving is a private matter. That is why many stewardship churches do not release these donors' names and their contributions.)

Accountability means that we must put up a system that lessens slipups, thwarts inappropriate behaviors, and prevents the chance of anyone or a cabal from controlling God's money for their nefarious interests. The church must observe prescribed accounting practices and cook up a bona fide system of checks and balances. By assigning distinct responsibilities to volunteers and employees, we ensure that the bad eggs cannot harm the church without others intervening. In practice, it means designating different people to do specific work, such as collecting the money, counting it, recording the transaction in a ledger, making receipts, depositing the money in a bank, holding the bankbook, signing checks, and auditing the reports.

Double trouble comes to those who centralize financial power. The preeminent practice is for the pastor to assign to the Delta Force the responsibility of managing the church finances. In this arrangement, it is the Delta Force who makes the budget and apportions the funds according to the designated church priorities and expenditures—for example, care for the priest, services to the poor, ministry budgets, staff payroll and benefits, maintenance.

People will give generously if they trust the church leadership, if they know we spend the funds helping the poor and making disciples, and if they see we account for every centavo. To be transparent and accountable with God's money is the surest way to promote the bighearted participation of the people.

That said, transparency and accountability are the two vital cornerstones in reinvigorating our churches.

Honor Good Stewards

One of the most used techniques in behavior modification is positive reinforcement. The drill is to reward desirable behaviors so that they will reoccur in the future.

Positive reinforcement can come in many forms—awards, spoken acknowledgments, special mentions, and posting their stories on social media platforms and bulletin boards. *Acknowledge and honor the early adopters and exemplars of stewardship to create momentum.*

When done properly and regularly, it signifies to the parishioners that stewardship is now the church's highest priority, and good stewards are valued and celebrated in this alternative church model.

Create a Parish Database

A profound disadvantage of being a large church is the difficulty of communicating with her members. The new crop of telecommunication technologies, like emails, social media platforms, and text messaging make this hitherto titanic task doable.

To ride high atop these opportunities, however, the pastor needs a database—a computerized collection of information covering his parishioners' names, addresses, emails, and cellphone numbers. Some of the forward-looking and clever pastors used the campaign to roll out the pledges to take care of this sordid business.

As a result, they found themselves well positioned to lead their flocks into the digital age.

Yearly Pledge Renewal

The best practice is to renew the pledges every year. This is to give the parishioners opportunities to level up their commitments on prayer, service, and giving.

An effective approach is to let the parishioners start where they are, which often means at a level that is too small to fail.

Do not be dismayed if the initial pledges seem paltry by your standards. Starting small is a much better scheme than to strong-arm them to bite off more than they can chew. *How can you expect someone who has not donated a single peso his entire life to keep a pledge to donate 10 percent of his income to the church?*

We are not living in a fanciful idealistic realm filled with angels. We are in the real world filled with ruthless, steely men holding close every centavo. That is the starting line in this marathon.

Consider again our mantra that radical change proceeds from the slow aggregation of incremental improvements. Give the neophytes the leeway to start their stewardship expedition with baby steps. Give them the time they need to grow and increase in faith.

But do not allow them to stay in that *too small to fail* framework all their lives either. As they grow spiritually, we should encourage them to ramp up their praying, serving, and giving. Stewardship should stretch us. It should help us go beyond our comfort zones and familiar havens. It should challenge and dare us to be better.

By asking the faithful to renew their pledges annually, we give them the opportunity to bump up their commitments so they may grow in stewardship.

The HOW of PLEDGING

Rolling Out the Pledges

The best practice is to use the Stepladder Approach—focus on one habit at a time.

Start with the Stewardship of Time. Once you have locked prayer up and it has gained a life of its own, introduce the Stewardship of Talent. When the habit of serving is mainstreamed in the church's life, only then do you roll out the Stewardship of Treasure.

In practical terms, it takes from three to six months for a habit to take root. Following this pattern, it takes nine to eighteen months for a church to bring to bear all the stewardship commitments on Time, Talent, and Treasure.

Why the seemingly lackadaisical discharge of pledges?

Changing habits is hard. If you ask people to make too many changes, you will fail. It is best to focus on one habit at a time. Make sure that the new habit sticks first by giving it a few months to take root before you ask the congregation to embark on a new habit.

That is why you'll do much better if you **make haste slowly!**

Concerning the target audience, the best practice is to cast wider and wider nets until you cover the entire parish. Start with the pastor, Parish Pastoral Council (PPC), and the leaders of the Ministries and LOMA. After that, set out for the members. Thenceforward, focus on the leaders and members of the chapels and BECs.

It is only after all the leaders are pledging that you open the hatchway for the rest of the congregation's participation.

The logic behind this approach is that **we are more likely to act magnanimously if we know our leaders in the church are *authentic and practice what they preach*.** We don't want to be jerked around, so we investigate and see how our leaders are doing. If we see that our leaders are praying, giving, and serving, then we follow their lead. If we see that our leaders are all talk and no action, we also follow suit!

That is human nature—we are sensitively aware of what others around us are doing.

Under any circumstances, the pastor and church leaders must always serve as genuine models who faithfully embrace their stewardship commitments.

Handing Out the Pledge Cards

The best practice is to hand out the pledge cards at the end of the basic Stewardship Workshops. Those ready to make commitments can fill out the pledge forms and offer them at the Eucharistic celebration usually held after the workshops.

The other popular method is to distribute the pledge cards to the faithful at Sunday Mass. I hear tell, however, that churches that do this do so only after they have saturated the entire parish with stewardship education. It is not a suitable form to ask people to make stewardship commitments without having undergone proper formation.

Collecting the Pledge Cards

Regarding how the cards are collected, all stewardship commitments of Time, Talent, and Treasure are turned in at the offertory. We place a collection box before the altar where the people can give the cards and envelopes as their offerings. This practice underlines the actuality that these pledges are promises we make to God.

It is the method of the Stewardship of Treasure that is atypical and singular in its ways.

While *Stewardship of Time and Talent pledge cards are turned in once a year*, the common run is for pledgers to *offer the Stewardship of Treasure cards **weekly at Sunday Mass***. The pledge cards on Treasure are also *envelopes* and not sheets of paper as are the Time and Talent pledges. Each pledger's name and contact details as well as his weekly financial offerings are written on the front of the envelope.

Returning the Envelopes

Regarding how to return the emptied envelopes back to the pledgers, the widespread practice is to do that before Sunday Mass. The custom is to lay out the alphabetically sorted envelopes on a table at the front entrance of the church for pick up. New envelopes are also made available for those who lost theirs and first-timers who want to start regular giving.

Some parishes ask their leaders to go house-to-house to get the Stewardship of Treasure commitment envelopes and turn them over to the parish. I am very much against this practice despite its pluses on systematized efficiency. It needlessly exposes the leaders to the risks faced by all who handle other people's money. It also takes away from their roles as spiritual heads, as they have to devote a substantial slab of their time to gather the donations week in and week out.

A case in point: A well-respected church leader was subjected to ruinous gossip because there was a discrepancy between the amount written on the envelope she collected and what was, actually, inside. After an official investigation, it turned out that the donor unwittingly enclosed the wrong amount on the envelope. Unfortunately, loose lips have already tarnished the leader's reputation.

PARTING SHOT

The church is an institution with systems, traditions, policies, and procedures. But she is, foremost, the people of God.

One reason most efforts to renew the church hit the skids is that church builders often fail to change human behaviors and habits. They may get the actions of rebuilding the institution right —strategic planning, effective programs, proper administration— but if they cannot change the people, their hard work often comes to grief.

Expressly, **integral renewal involves rehabilitating the insti-**

tution and transforming the people.

For changing the habits of the congregation, the stewardship pledge is a tool that is second to none. Without it, our lofty ambition to revitalize the house of the Lord is but a shot in the dark.

TAKEAWAYS

The fifth step in building a stewardship church that loves the poor is to **roll out the pledges.**

Why Do We Put Up Stewardship Pledges?

To help the faithful cultivate the habits of prayer, service, and giving. All this so they can transform themselves and become committed Catholics and genuine disciples of Christ.

What Are the Pledges?

- Stewardship of Time (or Prayer)—pledge to spend more time in prayer
- Stewardship of Talent (or Service)—commit to share our talents with the church
- Stewardship of Treasure—vow to donate regularly to the church

Best Practices

- Put up institutional mechanisms to take in new volunteers and resources.
- Apply principles of transparency and accountability.
- Honor good stewards.
- Create a database of parishioners.
- Renew the pledges yearly.

How Do We Roll Out the Pledges?

1. Start with Stewardship of Time, follow up with Talent, and finish with Treasure.

2. Start with the parish leaders in the center and periphery before setting your sights on the congregation.

STEP 6: SHIFT THE CHURCH'S GRAVITY TO FAVOR THE POOR

HOLD FOR A MOMENT in your hands what you have made so far—a praying, serving, and giving church that makes disciples. If properly hatched, this new stewardship church should trounce, quick as a wink, the many other past incarnations of your house of worship.

You took your church from a season when leaves withered and fell and brought her to a season when the leaves grew back and flourished. You faced towering challenges along the way, but you persevered and plowed through until you hit pay dirt. No two ways about it, you and your Team deserve a chorus of congratulations and praise!

Still, we are not yet through. There is the pending matter of shifting the church's gravity to favor the exploited and marginalized.

Why does this make a difference? Why is a stewardship church minus the preferential love for the poor close but no cigar?

To help you make sense of it, let's meander back to 1991 and the Second Plenary Council of the Philippines that was presided by Archbishop Leonardo Legaspi. The Council deliberated and put to the wringer this question: **How can the Church be a credible evangelizer given the pastoral context of the Philippines?**

After praying and racking their brains for a month, the Council

—which is a complete representation of the Philippine Church— arrived with this response: **By becoming a church that is faithful to its mission of** *integral evangelization.*

Figuring out the constitutive dimension of a church renewed is effortful and messy, like nailing jelly to the wall. But the Second Plenary Council pulled it off. It singled out integral evangelization as what the doctor ordered for the Philippine Church.

But what is this strange potion?

Integral evangelization is the espousal of both the *eternal* **and** *temporal* **dimensions of the Good News.** It is an embracement of the gospel truth that eternal salvation is *not* separate from human liberation; that the fullness of the kingdom fulfilled in Jesus's second coming is *not* separate from the "here but not yet" kingdom of peace, justice, truth, and love.

According to the Council, to announce the Gospel of Jesus as salvific, in a church where many of our brothers and sisters are as poor as dirt, she must become a proponent of human liberation. The Catholic Church must stand up for the poor as they are the primary casualties of a world entangled in an infernal race to the bottom. She must take up the struggles of the poor and turn the tables on the societal contrivances that prevent the excluded and oppressed from realizing their fullest personal and communitarian blossoming as sons and daughters of God.

To follow Jesus in the mission, the church must be a counterforce that smothers the rising tide of poverty, ignorance, oppression, injustice, and corruption. *To be a credible evangelizer in the Philippines, the church must, therefore, become a church that opts for the poor—a Church of the Poor.* Here is what the Council said:

"The Church seeks to transform the whole fabric of society according to the values of the Kingdom and Christ." (*PCP II*, no. 192)

That is a stunning proposition!

It is extraordinary because it uses the Gospel as the integrating principle to pursue human development, justice, peace, and care for the earth. Furthermore, **it designates this *upliftment of the poor* as the Push Goal—the domino tile that sets things in motion—to realize God's kingdom,** or a new world order where we care for each other and all creation.

The Second Plenary Council describes its vision of God's kingdom like this:

"That all may have life, we shall have to create a free nation: where human dignity and solidarity are respected and promoted; where moral principles prevail in socio-economic life and structure; where justice, love, and solidarity are the inner driving forces of development.

We shall have to build a sovereign nation: where every tribe and faith are respected; where diverse tongues and traditions work together for the good of all; where membership is a call to participation and involvement and leadership a summon to generous service.

Ours will have to be a people in harmony with one another through unity in diversity; in harmony with creation, and in harmony with God.

Ours shall be a civilization of life and love." (*PCP II Final Document*, nos. 253–255)

To stuff it nice as pie, the vision of a church renewed in the Philippines is one that goes to bat for the excluded and oppressed. The Council sees the liberation of the poor as the principal thoroughfare to realize

1. A transformed church
2. The kingdom of God

HOW DO WE BECOME THE CHURCH OF THE POOR?

The Second Plenary Council points the way so we do not make a dog's breakfast of it.

"Our vision of the Church as communion, participation, and mission, about the Church as priestly, prophetic and kingly people, and a Church of the Poor—a church that is renewed is today finding expression in one ecclesial movement. This is the movement to foster Basic Ecclesial Communities." (*PCP II,* no. 137)

There it is, the high sign and nod from the Second Plenary Council of the singular importance of small Christian communities or Basic Ecclesial Communities (BECs) in the renewal of our churches. It is down that long road we must go if we want to reach our desired landing place.

Remember our vision of the church as **communion, participation, and mission?**

- How can we become a church marked by *communion* where we know, love, and help one another when the rich and the poor don't even know each other and have no relationship or bond?

- How can we turn into a church marked by *participation* where we share our prayer, talent, and treasure when the poor, the sick, the marginalized, and lapsed Catholics are uninvited and unwelcome in the house of the Lord?

- How can we grow into a church marked by *mission* where we preach the word of God in words and deeds when most of our people in the margins of society are uninstructed in the ways of a disciple?

Call to mind our vision of the church as **priestly, prophetic, and kingly people**.

- How can we become a church of God's people who take part in liturgical services and live a life of prayer when the poor and marginalized are unchurched? (Priestly)

- How can we turn into a church who proclaims love, truth, and justice and denounces social evil when the church does not lift a finger to help many of our brothers and sisters who are victims of social evil? (Prophetic)

- How can we mature into a church who takes part in activities that care for humanity and all of creation when we do not even take care of the sick, the poverty-stricken, and the unchurched in our parishes? (Kingly)

It may sound nutty as a fruitcake, but we do not have an apparatus in the church that can foster communion, participation, and mission better than the BECs. It is far and away the sharpest knife in our drawer.

But what are BECs?

BASIC ECCLESIAL COMMUNITIES

Basic Ecclesial Communities (BECs) "are small communities of Christians, usually of families who gather together around the Word of God and the Eucharist. These communities are united to their pastors but are ministered to regularly by lay leaders. The members know each other by name and share not only the Word of God and the Eucharist but also their concerns, both material and spiritual. They have a strong sense of belongingness and responsibility for one another" (*PCP II*, no. 138).

Let us pause for a moment to find the right notes on why BECs are vital to church renewal; why BECs are the bottom line and not a "like it or dump it affair."

Lay Organizations, Movements, and Associations (LOMA) and Ministries provide noble services that support apostolic endeavors. Catastrophically, they are often not inclined or configured to evangelize in the periphery. This is bitter pill to swallow, but it is the truth that is as ugly as a blobfish! How can they promote communion, participation, and mission when they run a mile to avoid the poor who live in our society's underbelly?

In case the pastor can influence the LOMA and Ministries to make disciples in the margins of society, can they help make a priestly, prophetic, and kingly people? The answer is, yes, they can. Unfortunately, they can only take in a few members. What about the heaps of people in the margins? Can the Ministries accommodate 1,000 recruits? Can the LOMA?

For that reason, they cannot do the job.

What about regular participation in Sunday services? Can this help make a priestly, prophetic, and kingly people? As a first step, yes. However, it still takes ongoing formation, involvement, and accompaniment to grease the wheel to roll towards Christian perfection.

So this pathway to holiness also cannot come up to snuff.

The BEC program provides the long-term formation, accompaniment, and involvement we need for Christian maturity to shine through. The program promotes communion, participation, and mission among neighbors through dialogue, religious celebrations, community gatherings, and formation activities. BEC can accommodate throngs of people and promote communal discernment and collaborative action.

In a word, **the BEC Program** *supports the people of God* **as they deal with the spiritual, political, economic, ecological, and social issues that bedevil their community; and** *helps the layperson* **fulfill her calling to bring about a civilization of life and love.**

BEC is what puts the periphery in the center of the map and what *draws the excluded inside the Catholic tent*. It makes disciples from people in the margins and enables them to man the frontline of the kingdom.

That is why this BEC Program is a big deal!

This brings us to the seventh step on how to build a stewardship church that loves the poor—**we must shift the gravity of the church to favor the poor**.

The Church of the Poor will not build herself—we must go all in to make this dream an actuality. This is now our new push goal, and the Delta Force should make sure that all roads in the parish lead to this destination.

THE FOUR BATTLEGROUNDS

This chapter is about

- ✓ **Aligning the church's priorities to the mission**
- ✓ **Creating or strengthening institutional mechanisms**

The other battlegrounds are

- Changing the habits of the faithful
- Putting a culture in place that makes the change permanent

NEW PUSH GOAL

A word to the wise, do not embark on this new endeavor unless stewardship is firmly planted in the church and is in strapping, good shape. It may take a year or two for that to happen, but it is best to wait lest this new endeavor messes everything up. As we can't even walk and whistle at the same time, it makes sense to keep this new priority of building the Church of the Poor under wraps until stewardship is in the pink and flourishing in your parish.

Now, onward to building this church that uplifts the poor!

We have been down this path a few times before, so you know the drill. The opening salvo is to make an implementation plan that clarifies the *Why, What & How.* We must secure this under our belts before we lift a finger to lick the church into shape.

The WHY of SHIFTING GRAVITY

Why shift the gravity of the church to favor the poor?

We do this to become a Church of the Poor—a church that loves the poor and liberates them from spiritual and material poverty.

Our goal is to build a church marked by communion, participation, and mission. We want a church made up of priestly, prophetic, and kingly people. We yearn for a church that works with the poor so they can lift themselves from poverty. We desire a church that safeguards the church's resources and blessings to benefit the poor. We seek a church that takes on the poor's struggles and advocacies. We dream of a church that opts for the poor and makes the poor her primary evangelizers. We long for **a church where the rich and the poor are one—a community of disciples.**

Unless the pastor and Delta Force lead the charge to realize this singular goal, and unless the PPC, Ministries, and LOMA zero in on building a church that loves the poor as the synthesizing focus of the mission, we will forever remain an exclusive church for the saved and the few.

That is what's at stake here!

We are now playing for all the marbles.

The WHAT of SHIFTING GRAVITY

Vital Elements in Gravitational Shift

WHAT can we do to realize this lofty ambition? Here are the pioneers' four best practices to build a stewardship church that loves the poor:

Strengthen BECs or Small Christian Communities

The good news is that most parishes in the Philippines have BECs, so we are not starting from scratch. The hitch is in the BECs' quality and caliber—most cannot go beyond the model of praying communities.

That is the millstone around the BEC program's neck. It can make prayer groups in a flash, but it is all thumbs in manifesting the prophetic and kingly demeanors of God's people. The root of the predicament is that most BEC organizers and leaders lack the competencies and experience necessary to overcome structural evil—power arrangements, laws, institutions, and policies that oppress and exploit the poor.

Lacking sophistication in dealing with developmental issues, the blind impulse of most wide-eyed BEC leaders is to deal with poverty by grandiose economic projects. Because small Christian communities do not have the money to underwrite enormous projects (e.g., livelihood, housing, scholarships, cooperatives), they often apply for financial support from the parish. The trouble with this is when the parish cannot bankroll these grand schemes, the ambition to better the community loses steam, and the BECs backslide to their usual quiddity as praying communities.

The pioneers who figured it out and made BECs of the first water did not rely on parish funds. They instead gathered the talents and material resources of the people and brought these small blessings to bear on the issues at hand. As the communities have limited material resources and experience, they teed off on small, manageable projects before they sank their teeth into more ambitious and giant undertakings later.

Instead of kicking off with high-flying livelihood projects or credit cooperatives, they suitably began with a simple *paluwagan* (an informal group savings and rotating credit scheme) whereby people can have access to money in times of emergencies; instead of big-ticket feeding programs, they taught the people container gardening to grow their vegetables; instead of establishing and maintaining high-cost Parish Emergency Response Teams, they rolled out disaster preparedness workshops so community members can help one another in times of calamities.

The wellspring of the problem is that we often use catechists as our BEC program organizers and overseers. These heroes are masterly proficient in religious instruction but unseasoned in dealing with developmental issues, such as corruption, ecological disasters, human rights violations, and poverty. You cannot fault these catechist organizers for missing the mark because they are ill-equipped to win this war. They do the best they can and go by their best light. Unfortunately, and it pains for me to say this, they do not have the right stuff to cut the mustard.

The best practice of the pioneers is to **hire organizers and BEC program managers who can deal with the many socioeconomic and political issues that put down the disadvantaged communities.** As a second alternative, the parish can create *Immersion Programs* where existing BEC organizers and leaders learn the meat and potatoes of community organizing and development work from civil society organizations.

The bottom line is we need BEC leaders and managers who are

fit for purpose, who carry a big bag of tricks that include expertise and savvy in development work or human liberation.

That is the way out of this cul-de-sac.

Any other way is to whistle in the wind.

Realign the LOMA and Ministries to Support BECs

This huge undertaking is a play in two acts.

The opening gun is to prevail upon the LOMA and Ministries' leaders and members to join up with the small Christian communities or BECs in their neighborhoods. The next volley is to ask the LOMA and Ministries to retool or realign some of their services toward the blossoming of the BECs.

There is not much chop and substance to integral renewal if the Ministries and LOMA do not throw their support behind the BECs. Some pioneers, therefore, asked the leaders and members of the lay organizations to join up with the BECs in their neighborhoods. Even though some leaders refused to take the plunge because they already have too much on their plates, most took it in good part.

Being the parish spearhead—with vast experience running pastoral programs under their belts—these brood of leaders can use their competencies to push the BECs to reach their highest ground.

The other common maneuver is to ask the LOMA and Ministries to put their backs behind the new push goal of shifting the gravity of the church to favor the poor. What can the LOMA and Ministries come up with to meet this new priority? Can they redirect some of their *existing services* to the BECs? Or can they knock together *new services* to breathe life into the BECs?

More often than not, the Ministries and LOMA come through. They get in the act and get cracking to help the BECs.

Put Up New Church Programs and Services That Help the Poor

Poverty reduction is at the heart of the struggle for human liberation. It is, thus, crucial that we know what we mean by poverty. If we define it in monetary terms, such as lack of income to pay for basic needs, then our mitigation efforts will converge around income generation.

If we, however, define **poverty as a** *deprivation of opportunities to live a decent life*, **this jostles us to see poverty as a vast landscape with social, political, economic, and ecological dimensions.** This standpoint impels us to roll out a profusion of varied services—education, health, housing, and community building, to name a few—to end poverty in all its forms and manifestations!

Our pioneers' best practice is to organize the poor in sectors, like single parents, overseas workers, persons with disabilities, LGBTQ, women, factory workers, and farmers. Then they rig out an assortment of spiritual, physical, economic, psychological, and political services to meet the sectors' respective needs.

There is much to nitpick about the pioneers' efforts at poverty reduction. There is, for example, a lack of thought on what specific dimension of poverty to focus on, and a sparsity of formal evaluations. Even so, I don't want to make a song and dance number about it because I see that all of this is driven by a pure heart that wants to lessen the misery of people in dire straits.

Know also that the churches are not civil society organizations. My hat off to the churches for doing what they can to fight poverty despite their lack of expertise in development work. Long may you all live!

I reserve my denunciations to churches that do nothing to help the poor—you are all mouth and no trousers. You are as useless to the poor as handbrakes on a bamboo raft.

"He who oppresses a poor man insults his Maker,
but he who is kind to the needy honors him." (Proverbs 14:31)

Enshrine "Love for the Poor" and "Stewardship" in the Mission Statements

Vision and Mission Statements help the faithful know the purpose and reason their parish church exists. They reveal who we are, what we do, and where we are going. This makes Vision-Mission

Statements indispensable navigational aids to setting institutional priorities, allocating resources, and ensuring that everyone is rowing towards the same shore.

Vision Statements focus on desired goals or end states. They describe how the church will look when it achieves its mission. The best practice of the pioneers is to keep it short enough to remember but long enough to describe the purpose. Here is an example of such a Vision Statement:

> *To promote life in its fullness so we may all be*
> *responsible stewards of humankind and all creation.*

It is concise, yet it communicates the transcendent goal of the church in a way that easily sticks in your mind. "Life in its fullness," however, is a church jargon that might need some explaining. It means a life filled with socioeconomic, ecological, and spiritual blessings. It is the positive result or outcome of human liberation.

Because the common run is to fasten the local church's vision to God's plan for salvation, most Vision Statements are thus timeless and unchanging, even when the local church amends its mission and strategies.

Ergo, our focus on the Mission Statement.

A Mission Statement contains three things: What we do, how we do it, and for whom. They are beacons of light that help the Ministries and LOMA work in concert to achieve a common purpose. They also convey to the parishioners what their church is passionate about and what it strives for.

The best practice is to enshrine *love for the poor* and *stewardship* in the church's Mission Statement so the faithful know that these are the two inviolable aspirations of their parish. Here is an example Mission Statement that does that:

> *To make every person in the parish a disciple of Christ whose*
> *way of life is marked by prayer, service, giving, and love for the poor.*
>
> *We accomplish this by promoting stewardship as*
> *the principal spirituality in our church, and by building BECs.*

Key Result Areas

Let us now translate the best practices listed above into Key Result Areas (KRAs) and success indicators. Without a way of telling the state we're in—if we are lagging, running in place, or turning a corner—we will soon end up in tatters.

From these KRAs, the Delta Force must extract and hash out the specific *quantitative* and *qualitative* indicators of success.

1. A strong and vibrant BEC Program

The devil here is in the details. The Delta Force must chew over what they mean by a strong and vibrant BEC. We shall then derive the success indicators from the operational understanding.

- *Is a vibrant BEC Program about total membership?* An example success indicator is when 20% of total parishioners belong to BECs.

- *Is it about standardized organizational mechanisms and processes?* A plausible indicator for this is when 50% of BECs are meeting regularly, or 80% of BECs have elected officials.

- *Is it about manifesting the prophetic and kingly dimensions?* A sample indicator is when 25% of BECs are tackling community issues.

2. Ministries and LOMA have realigned their services to the BEC

Once again, the Delta Force will need to carefully deliberate what this means to figure out this KRA's success indicators.

- *Is it about the success of persuading the Ministries and LOMA leaders to join the BECs?* Perhaps the success indicator is when 75% of the members of LOMA and Ministries join their local BECs.

- *Or is it about the Ministries and LOMA developing new services to nurture BECs?* Then a plausible indicator is when 80% of LOMA and Ministries have put up at least one new service program to help the BECs.

3. The church has many new services to help the poor

- *Is it about the services made available to the sectors?* Show the services you want to provide—psychological, physical, legal, and so forth.

- *Is it about the number of poor people served?* Peg a number to your indicator, e.g., 1,000 beneficiaries served this year.

4. "Love for the poor" and "stewardship" are enshrined in the Mission Statement

This is by far the easiest of the lot to make a success indicator for. *Love for the poor* and *stewardship* is incorporated in the Mission statement.

The HOW of SHIFTING GRAVITY

The *7 Steps* to a Church That Loves the Poor

The first part you have gone through is *The 7 Steps on How to Build a Stewardship Church*. To complete the circle, we now come to the second and final procedure: *The 7 Steps to Build a Church That Loves the Poor*. There are some variations in steps here, but the two procedures are like two peas in a pod—yes, there are differences, but they are so slight that they won't befuddle you.

What takes the biscuit is you've already built a stewardship church from scratch, therefore, you are now familiar with the routine on how to introduce change in the parish and make it stick.

So take your courage in both hands and sally forth!

Step 1. Sound the Alarm!

Step 2. Make *Strengthen the BECs* the Delta Team's New Push Goal

Step 3. Figure out the *Why, What & How* of BECs

Step 4. Launch a Massive BEC Formation Program

Step 5. Strengthen the BECs

Step 6. Realign LOMA and Ministries to Serve the BECs

Step 7. Make Stewardship the Dominant Church Culture

TAKEAWAYS

The sixth step in building a stewardship church that loves the poor is to **shift the gravity of the church to favor the poor**.

Why Do We Do This?

To realize our vision of the church

- as communion, participation, and mission
- as priestly, prophetic & kingly people
- as a Church of the Poor

What Are the Key Result Areas?

1. Vibrant BECs

2. Ministries and LOMA are serving the BECs

3. The church has new services for the poor

4. *The church's Mission Statement incorporates love for the poor and stewardship*

How Do We Go About Making This Change?

Step 1. Sound the Alarm!

Step 2. Make *Strengthen the BECs* the Delta Team's New Push Goal

Step 3. Figure out the *Why, What & How* of BECs

Step 4. Launch a Massive BEC Formation Program

Step 5. Strengthen the BECs

Step 6. Realign LOMA and Ministries to Serve the BECs

Step 7. Make Stewardship the Dominant Church Culture

STEP 7: MAKE STEWARDSHIP THE DOMINANT CHURCH CULTURE

LET US SIT STILL and orient ourselves to the moment. Let us muse over what we have done to prevail in **The Four Battle-grounds of Transformational Change**.

We have

✓ Spelled out and mainstreamed Stewardship and the Church of the Poor as our highest priorities

✓ Incorporated *Stewardship* and *Love for the Poor* in our official Mission Statement

✓ Strengthened organizational mechanisms and processes

- instituted the Delta Force as the main decision-making and implementing body of the church
- strengthened the BEC, stewardship, and formation programs
- realigned the organizations—Parish Pastoral Council (PPC), Lay Organizations, Movements, and Associations (LOMA), and Ministries—toward making disciples and serving the poor

✓ Put up the Stewardship Program to help the faithful develop the habits of prayer, service, giving, and love for the poor

To round it up and polish it off, we now come to the fourth area of contention:

✓ **Creating a stewardship culture that will dye the transformations in the wool**

A CULTURE IN LINE WITH MISSION

Most of our stewardship pioneer builders in the Philippines are unconversant in the academic meanings of culture. Nevertheless, they have the instinct and intuition to know in their bones that there are tangibles (i.e., organizational mechanisms, programs, buildings) as well as intangibles (i.e., symbols, rituals, stories, and values) in the church that determine her well-being, proficiency, and attainments.

There are complex definitions of culture that involve an interlacing of control systems, organizational structures, power hierarchies, paradigms, rituals, symbols, and mythic stories. For our purposes, a simple definition of culture as *the way we do things or the way of life shared by the church community* will suffice.

That was enough for the pioneer builders to get by; it should be enough for us.

The WHY of STEWARDSHIP CULTURE

The name of the game is to understand that although culture is invisible like the wind, when it is aligned to the mission, church affairs proceed smoothly and rapidly. Alternatively, when culture is opposed to the mission, church interactions proceed listlessly.

The rundown for church builders is not a scholarly knowledge of culture but a practical, working understanding of it to help them navigate two pressing questions:

1. What kind of culture nurtures the stewardship church that loves the poor?
2. How do you change church culture?

The answer to the first problem could lead us down the proverbial rabbit hole if we are not careful. We must therefore be watchful and keep things as simple as possible. This is, however, easier said than done because the new culture the pioneers adopted was a complex patchwork of

- Assumptions (e.g., kingdom of God, Jesus as the Good Shepherd, Church of the Poor)
- Values (e.g., identity, gratitude, trust, justice, and love for the poor)
- Cultural artifacts (e.g., clean churches conducive to worship, tip-top communication facilities)

How do you describe this amalgamation and peg it under a single label? An ambitious task indeed since this new culture is more of vapor than a phenomenon with corporeality. The best I can do is to present the five undiluted specimens that make up this new variety. Perhaps by revealing their substances, you can distinguish, understand, and bottle them up to use in your parishes.

The WHAT of STEWARDSHIP CULTURE

The Stewardship Culture

The mishmash of the five cultures below is the essence of the new culture that we should put in place to ensure the continuing success of the stewardship church that loves the poor. For our purposes, let us call this new hybrid "Stewardship Culture" even though we know this one goes a long way beyond the bounds of what a traditional stewardship culture signifies.

It is a chimera made up of stewardship, love for the poor, service excellence, collaboration, and learning by trial and error all rolled into one new culture species.

Unlike the chimera of mythology, this new culture is not illusory and can be brought into existence. Each one is peculiar, but we can blend and distill these five dissimilar spirits together into one.

Stewardship

As good church stewards, we take on the responsibility of making disciples. We must therefore work to help others develop the habits of prayer, service, giving, and love for the poor. This is the primary task entrusted to us all, but it falls heavily on the shoulders of leaders and church builders.

The leaders fulfill this duty by instituting Stewardship Programs of Prayer, Talent, and Treasure. In like manner, they carry it out by strengthening the BECs, LOMA, and Ministries for social action and services.

Love for the Poor

God's love for all of us who could not save ourselves propelled him to send his only begotten Son to die on the cross on our behalf. If there is anything we should get down pat from that, we too should have compassion for the needy and stone broke. *As recipients of unconditional love, let us watch over the impoverished and shunned and care for them the best way we can.*

> "If there is among you a poor man, one of your brethren, in any of your towns within your land which the Lord your God gives you, you shall not harden your heart or shut your hand against your poor brother, but you shall open your hand to him, and lend him sufficient for his need, whatever it may be." (Deuteronomy 15:7–8)

Service Excellence

It takes high-performing leaders to drive the church to institutional excellence. They must enforce the highest standards on programs, church leaders, and actions to ensure that the church meets her principal aim of making disciples who care for all of creation.

They can accomplish this through the extensive use of implementation plans and performance evaluations. It is by regularly subjecting actions, programs, and personnel through inquiry— *What happened? What went well, and why? What did not go well, and why? What do we do next?*—that pushes the church programs and actions to the next level.

Collaboration

When leaders with varying traits, experiences, and skills come together to chart the course of the church, they can resolve even longstanding problems that prevent the church from achieving her highest ambitions and goals.

By what method? By bringing varied perspectives in talking the problem through and exploring the alternative solutions available. The more eyes examining the problem the easier it is to spot the land mines; the more intellects looking for solutions, the easier it is to discover the breakthroughs. *A culture that celebrates collaboration also lifts the team's morale and strengthens the sense of community.*

The leaders can pull this off by running the organizational meetings as roundtables, encouraging thinking outside the box, and emboldening everyone to build on other's ideas.

Learning by Trial and Error

The creative process of solving issues and problems is a journey that involves a lot of slipups, missteps, and failures. For the church to prevail and prosper, her leaders must not come apart when they encounter failures. They must endure defeats and continue their forward momentum. They must do their best to resolve the issue at hand using various means until they discover the correct pathway that leads to victory.

That is the frame of mind that this culture of learning by trial and error nurtures. **Embracing the mentality of failing early, you mitigate the costs and the risks as well as prepare yourself to face bigger challenges in the future.**

This is the attitude we need to succeed in the long haul.

Your leaders promote this culture by how they run their regular organizational meetings. They likewise encourage the use of research and the pilot approach in implementing decisions and pay special attention to the view that, if they fail often, they will succeed sooner.

The cultures of *collaboration* and *learning by trial and error* are crucial in addressing the issues of power in the parish. Through the extensive use of the two, the church can create a flatter against a hierarchical and authoritarian church. They are necessary vehicles for the wholesale development and release of your lay leaders' gifts and talents.

STEWARDSHIP CULTURE MADE ALIVE

The last step in building a stewardship church that loves the poor is to **make this newfangled *Stewardship Culture* the dominant culture of the parish.** The pastor and all key church leaders must embrace and promote it. It must be operational in the life of the LOMA and Ministries. It must live and breathe in the small Christian communities. It must preside and reverberate in the lives of the ordinary parishioner.

It is only by dousing the entire parish in *Stewardship Culture* that we can say we have transformed the church into a praying, serving, and giving church that loves the poor.

The HOW of STEWARDSHIP CULTURE

The Five Indirect Ways to Cultural Change

Let us now move forward to the second question that plagued the pioneer builders: How do we change the culture?

Considering that culture is a phenomenon with its intricate dynamics and momentum, academicians say we cannot change it directly. Why? Because cultural change happens slowly and naturally in the wake of change in the organization, people's habits and beliefs, and contexts. As it is a wheel within a wheel in the overall renewal of the institution, it means you cannot change culture by direct actions, like, let us say, issuing organizational edicts and decrees.

Cultural change is like the pursuit of happiness. We cannot attain happiness by coming after it directly. But we can get to it in a roundabout way by the pursuing good health, a keen mind, a rewarding career, and supportive and loving relationships.

In the same manner, we cannot change culture by pursuing cultural change straightforwardly. But we can do so by indirect means. Below are the top five indirect ways the pioneers use to bring about cultural change:

By Modeling Stewardship

The fact is, people are examining church leaders on their authenticity. They are on the lookout if words match deeds, if proclamations match actions.

To be an effective stewardship promoter, a church leader must therefore be the real thing—an authentic steward. She must live stewardship, speak stewardship, teach stewardship 24/7. Stewardship cannot be like a fashionable shirt a leader puts on when she goes to church and then takes off when she goes home. She must bake stewardship into her person. It must be her way of life and her way of being.

If not, people will smell the duplicity and declare stewardship but an elaborate scheme to pry money from their wallets. *This is why it is imperative that the pastor and all church leaders must also faithfully pledge a portion of their treasure to the church* atop their commitments on time and talent.

How can they ask the people to give to God when they do not?

By What We Choose to Measure and Keep Track of

Why do we measure things, events, or performances?

We do this to keep an eye out for *that which is most significant to us*. If the most significant thing dips in performance, then we intervene in a flash to invigorate it; if it stays level and flat, we want to know what we can do to help it grow; if it mounts upwards, we keep our hands on the wheel to make sure it stays the course.

If the pastor and the Delta Force are measuring the growth of the small Christian communities, such as the quality of services for the poor and the number of street masses celebrated, it signals to the parishioners that this is our priority. If we only measure and monitor the amount of money coming in, then that is an arm-wave to the community that we are only preoccupied with cold hard cash.

We change the way things are done by what we choose to pay attention to, by what we measure, and by what we choose to improve.

By the Leaders We Choose

Are the people in charge of the church made up of middle-class, educated males? Are the poor and the unlettered denied superintendence of the ministries? Are the organizations run by matrons and graybeards? Do we appoint martinets and hard taskmasters to lead key initiatives and undertakings? Or do we empower people who have high emotional intelligence but cannot get things done?

Without saying a word, the Delta Force and the pastor speak volumes about the leaders they choose. Do they choose based on availability? Compliant disposition? Wealth? Political connections? Excellent communication skills? Critical thinking?

I dove into this in *Step 2: Build a Delta Force Team* and advised you to pick a mix of leaders who are Doers, Thinkers, People Connectors, and Influencers.

In a perfect world, the normal run is to consider an aspirant's character, competence, and commitment before you appoint him to a leadership position. More often than not, we are constrained to pick imperfect leaders who may be worthy in one aspect but diddly in another. As a practical corrective, the church must therefore provide formation that is continual and never-ending.

That, too, says a lot.

By Where We Put Resources

For a program or activity to succeed, it needs ample human and financial resources.

To say, for example, that the formation program and small Christian communities take precedence over other concerns in the church and then not give these initiatives the financial support and the notable leaders they need to flourish is pure hogwash.

We can deceive people by our pronouncements, but financial budgets never lie. We can sidetrack people by our proclamations, *but where we assign our best and brightest leaders and where we put our money reveal what we deem important*—they bring to light our real priorities.

To tilt the culture towards a stewardship church that loves the poor, the Delta Force should allocate funds and talents to programs and activities that make disciples, such as stewardship programs, BECs, formation, and social action.

By Who We Reward and Praise

The rituals of honoring exemplars and role models of stewardship go a long way in consolidating the transformational change we advocate in the parish. That is why the pioneer builders devise many ways to celebrate people who epitomize the disciple's way of life—a life of praying, serving, giving, and preferential love for the poor.

These rituals may involve special awards, citations, thank you notes, special mentions, or designed religious ceremonies. They are all important communal activities that draw us closer together, inspire us, and show us whom to emulate to become good disciples.

The best practice is to craft a basket of recognition and awards. Honor old and young stewards. Honor rich and poor stewards. Honor men and women stewards. Honor church leaders and ordinary parishioners. Honor the Ministries. Honor the Movements, Organizations, and Associations. Honor the Delta Force Team. Honor the PPC. Honor the pastor.

This convention creates a culture that *praises and celebrates*

discipleship. **It promotes a way of life that** *appreciates and rewards spiritual breakthroughs.*

Culture, or how we do things, is not what we claim we believe or how we aspire to behave. Culture is but the repeating patterns of assumptions, values, and behaviors that prevail in the church; and, they continue to persist because we incentivize, reward, and reinforce these patterns.

Let us reward discipleship. Let us honor people who pray, serve, give, and love the poor out of gratitude for all the blessings they have received in their lives.

A SEND-OFF

At this point in your church renewal adventure, you have put together an alternative church model that makes disciples and cares for the poor.

Good job!

I pray you have narrowed the gap between what you want to do with your life with what you have done so far. I pray you have helped people find meaning in theirs.

Yet this is not the end of the road.

There is still the forward journey to ensure that this church sticks to her guns in the face of severe hardships, challenges, and provocations. To succeed, you will again need the Delta Force, willpower, skill, and God's blessing. Hopefully, your appetite for the mission will compel you to take on this challenge with relish.

Bon voyage.

God bless you.

Happy landing!

TAKEAWAYS

The seventh step in building a stewardship church that loves the poor is to **make stewardship the dominant church culture.**

Why Do We Change the Culture?

To fix in place the priorities, organizational mechanisms, and new habits of the people that we introduced. By this means, we preserve the stewardship church that loves the poor and ensure that she keeps well into the future.

What Culture Should We Promote?

A *Stewardship Culture* that is a mixture of the ways of stewardship, love for the poor, service excellence, collaboration, and learning by trial and error.

How Do We Change Culture?

We do this *directly* by transforming the organizational mechanisms and structures of the church, changing people's habits, and institutional priorities.

We do this *indirectly* by

- Modeling stewardship
- What we measure and control
- The leaders we choose
- Where we allocate our human and financial resources
- The people and organizations we reward and praise

PARTING WORDS

ONE CAN SAY THAT THE EXPERIENCE of the pioneer stewardship builders is an oddity. It stands in opposition to the common run where many church leaders learn to live with the institution by glossing over her errors, discrepancies, and abuses.

When you rummage around, you find that what the acquiescent majority reckons is not that the church cannot change but that church transformation is an arduous affair that brings a basketful of failures and disappointments. Rather than swim against the tide, they choose the easier route—they back down from the challenge, bow their heads, and let the fast-moving putrid current sweep them to where it will.

This is the fatalistic predilection and cynical view that the pioneer stewardship builders assailed and dispatched.

They showed us that with a pinch of smarts, a dash of divergent thinking, and a cup of never-give-up attitude, we can make the church better. The pioneers inspired us to conceive of an alternative church model—a stewardship church that loves the poor. They modeled how to give birth and care for this youngling church so she turns into a formidable protector of the downtrodden in this mad, mad world.

In light of that spirit and grace, my first parting thought for you is this: **Follow the footsteps of the stewardship pioneers and contend against any straying from the mission.** When the church is crooked, straighten her up; when the church is adrift, set her on the right course.

Our consciousness is how we define ourselves and what determines our destinies—if we think we are helpless, then we are helpless; if we think we are slaves, then we are slaves; if we think our place is to accept what is there, then we will never break lances to dispel the contracting forces of rot and corruption.

The renewal of our churches must not be but a passing stride in the eternal human march to the reign of God. **Let us do as the pioneers** *and dare to imagine a revitalized church.* Let us follow suit and build one that makes disciples devoted to human fellowship and care of the earth.

We are now amid a barking mad pandemic. The world and his wife agree that COVID-19 has gutted the church, and we will have to rehabilitate, reconstitute, and rebuild her when the disease has run its course.

Without doubt, this is the opportune time to plant seeds of genuine renewal.

Since we have to reconstruct the church anyway, why go back to a church that venerated cash flow and cared only for the saved few?

Let us knuckle down to put up a stewardship church that loves the poor. She is an able-bodied church that takes mission thoughtfully and passionately. She is a church that takes an active part in the kingdom's inbreaking by uplifting the poor.

Thanks to the pioneers' agency, this alternative model of God's house is in the saddle, all set to take the flock to better pastures.

Let's go and hit our straps!

ON EFFORT AND OUTCOMES

The second nutriment I leave you is this: **The ultimate touchstone of authentic humanity is presence and effort.**

When we say and do all, the key question to ask is not "Did you succeed at building a stewardship church that loves the poor?" but "What are the ways you made the church better?"

Sometimes, our hard work may not be enough to turn the church into a full-blooded stewardship church that loves the poor.

But do not get upset and sulk. Even if all we accomplished was to get the ball rolling in the right direction, we should still pat ourselves on the back. Remember, rarely are things worth doing accomplished in our lifetime. Thanks to our effort, we are now at least one step closer to the finish line.

But hold fast because, in the end, *it is the incremental improvements that usher earthshaking shifts and breakthroughs.*

So rather than dwell on completion, the central issue should be about presence and effort: When the church needed reanimation, did you show up and lend a hand? Did you harness and share your gifts and talents? Did you give it your best shot? Did you collaborate with fellow church builders? Did you believe in them? Did you accompany them on a journey impossible to accomplish alone?

In proper life, you win some and you lose some. This is how it is in the real world. Do not be mesmerized or besotted by the glitter of clear-cut outcomes and victories. After all, the key aspect in life is the journey, not the ultimate destination. We must therefore learn to befriend this cyclical rhythm of success and failure that marks our lives. We must allow it to bring self-sculpting beneficence to our beings.

Our presence and effort—this is all that God expects from us. Not victory at every battle, not success at every turn.

Do what you must do and hope that massive effort will take you from success to success. But if it doesn't, don't succumb to cynicism or disgruntlement. Reevaluate, replan, reapply yourself to your winged purposes and work like a Trojan!

Following this, there is nothing else you can do but breathe and trust God's plan.

THE CALL OF THE TIMES

We are beings *of* this time, *in* this time.

Our epoch is besieged with multifarious challenges, almost all of which are unprecedented. A global pandemic, deteriorating financial and global market systems, ocean rise, revolutions, perpetual wars, famines, droughts—and the list of debacles brought by human folly goes on and on.

The Catholic Church is also reeling from a boatload of crises. The institution is groggy and slap-punched like a boxer hit with a flurry of straights and crosses from widespread loss of faith, clerical sex abuse, financial impropriety, and failure to stand up to authoritarianism and human rights violations.

If we open a window to the world and take the panoramic view in, we would not be misguided to think that our modern civilization is on the brink of collapse and that humanity is on its last legs. In reverse, we would be delusional to believe that the catastrophes will resolve themselves and disappear like the mountain mists of Sagada at midday without massive and skillful human intervention.

What can we do?

As people of the pew, God calls us to revivify the church so that she can take part in the world's renewal.

The church is a powerful force that can be part of the problem or part of the solution. She can empower the poor, women, children, and the sick, or condemn them to the veiled, shadowy margins. She can uphold the integrity of creation or not say a word about mass extinction and climate change. She can uphold human dignity or not lift a finger to stop abuse and violations of our human rights.

To be a force for good, however, the church must be credible and authentic.

How can we fight corruption if we are corrupt? How can we be a champion of justice if we are unjust? How can we deplore infinite acquisitiveness that is impoverishing the natural world if we are avaricious and grasping? How can we ask others to step up when we easily cede and stand down?

We need a credible and authentic church working with governments, civil society organizations, and international institutions to find our way out of this existential debacle so we can emerge on the other side wiser and kinder. The Catholic Church and the other great world religions might not provide the direct solutions to the colossal problems of the world but they can provide the moral foundation for a world order aligned with our stewardship vision of peoples caring for one another and the earth.

The church can pitch into voicing a new global ethic—one based on a fundamental concurrence on values, norms, and standards. She can champion that all human beings have a dignity that corporations, governments, and social institutions must recognize and respect. She can endorse that no person, race, church, nation, or enterprise is beyond morality.

She can stand behind the truth that we are children of this earth —we are minerals, rivers, and trees who learned to love, dance, and sing.

That is the reason the renewal of our churches is of primal importance. Moreover, **the fate of the world depends on it**. And it is in this context that I give you this last bit of a morsel for your forward journey: **The time to act is now.**

If you are waiting for the perfect moment to act, if you are waiting for a still point in this turning world to commit, then the swirling, fast-moving events about us will get ahead of you, overwhelm you, and leave you behind. You can sit back on the sidelines and pray that things will get better and that the church and the world will land back on their feet.

Or you can roll up your sleeves and go to work.

The stewardship church that loves the poor will not build herself. *She needs you—your presence, your full-blooded effort, and your talent.* She beseeches you to jumpstart the forward movement of reform and rectification to make her better so she can become an effective player in the world's renewal.

This quest to revivify the church and the world might push us all to the breaking point of our beings. We must put up with the distress and hang tough. The devil's work is to break our spirits, and ours is to repudiate the evil one and carry on. We must rebuff the Archfiend with everything we have got. We must repulse him with the powerful arm of *joy* that we can only find from a life dedicated to a higher purpose.

Contrary to general belief, joy is not the absence of struggle and hardship; it is, rather, an inner elevation brought by our perseverance and focus to realize what is most essential in life—**renewing ourselves and our human institutions so that we may be good stewards of one another and all creation**.

The fate of the world hangs on a balance.

The fate of our world is in your hands.

ABOUT THE AUTHOR

Jose Luis Clemente

The author is a long-time Executive Director of the Socio-Pastoral Institute, a faith-based organization established in 1980 by prominent church people in the Philippines to help in the integral renewal of church and society.

He was a member of the Board of Directors of the International Catholic Stewardship Council (USA) and the Treasurer of the Association of Christian Institutes for Social Concern in Asia (Thailand).

Mr. Clemente is also a public speaker, an aspiring vegetarian, an award-winning documentary filmmaker, an erstwhile composer and musician, a writer, and a full-time husband.

Made in the USA
Middletown, DE
05 September 2023

37994927R00076